Advance Praise for
Raise the Child You've Got—
Not the One You Want

"In today's avalanche of parenting advice and pressures on children to conform, it is easy to be in conflict with your obstinate, difficult, or painfully shy child. Nancy Rose offers a wise and unique perspective on acceptance that makes parenting rewarding instead of an ongoing struggle. Follow her lead in accepting who your child is…you *and* your child will be so much happier."

—Susan Newman, Ph.D.,
author of *Little Things Long Remembered:
Making Your Children Feel Special Every Day*

Raise the Child You've GOT*

*Not the One You Want

Why Everyone Thrives When Parents
Lead with Acceptance

NANCY ROSE

BRAESIDE PRESS

1436 2nd Street #180

Napa, CA 94559

Publisher's Cataloging-In-Publication Data

Rose, Nancy, 1956-
    Raise the child you've got : not the one you want : why everyone thrives
when parents lead with acceptance / Nancy Rose.
        p. : ill. ; cm.
    Issued also as an ebook.
    Includes bibliographical references and index.
    ISBN: 978-0-9889038-0-7
    1. Parental acceptance. 2. Parenting. 3. Child rearing. I. Title.
HQ755.8 .R67 2013
649/.1   2013915176

Book Designer, Dorothy Carico Smith
Editor, Diane O'Connell
Contributing Writer and Researcher, Cristina Schreil

Printed in the United States of America

Author's note: Some names and identifying details have been changed to protect the privacy of individuals. In order to illustrate certain principles and techniques, some examples are composites of several children and families.

For the precious child in each of us

TABLE OF CONTENTS

Introduction

When did parenting come to require constant vigilance? Like most parents, you've made it a top priority to raise your children well, giving them all you can to ensure they have a safe, healthy life and a successful future.

But it isn't that easy. As if locked into an eternal hamster wheel of parental frustration, you find yourself constantly reminding your child to stop his temper tantrum, listen to your rules, play nice with others, stop talking back, finish his homework, stay off the computer, do his chores, apply to college...and act like an adult. Even when you're not caught in a relentless game of pushing and getting pushed back, you find yourself holding your breath each time the phone rings, filled with a sense of dread that it's the teacher, a playmate's parent, the principal...or the police.

"What happened to the sweet, beautiful baby I held in my arms?" you ask yourself. Perhaps you find yourself recalling your fantasy of how your child might be: driven and ambitious, or an artistic soul like you; in all cases, accomplishing feats left and right that admittedly would cast a bright glow your way.

You remember when your child idolized you, and wish it were still the case. You hear the warnings from parents of older kids, and you dread the day when your child morphs into a tempestuous teen who hardly speaks to you. Will you ever see eye to eye again? You're starting to see the truth in the saying, "Small children, small problems; big children, big problems."

You signed up for parenthood, not years of playing referee in your own home.

Like many parents, you might have hit the books. You might have even enrolled in workshops, desperately trying to get a handle on the problems between you and your child. You've tried playing bad cop, saying lines like, "Because I'm the parent and I say so." You've tried urging your shy toddler out of her shell, printed chore charts in attempts to get a hold of your son's laziness, or joined support groups for similarly dismayed parents of pre-teen daughters. At times, you've felt like you're approaching a breakthrough. But then, suddenly, you're back at square one, over and over and over again, as if you're Bill Murray's character in the movie *Groundhog Day*. Why is it impossible to make headway? Why is your child at such a distance, or at such odds with you? Why do the same issues continue to resurface?

With the litany of parenting advice everywhere you turn, your confusion is hardly surprising. Before writing this book, I searched online for "Parenting Books"— the search yielded over 7,000 results. And, once I started reading, I began to witness the very confusion today's parents experience. How, for instance, can one parenting book, written by an expert in his field, negate the very advice of another book written by someone who is just as qualified? "Do this," they say, "But, oh gosh, *never* do *that!*" Sure, one thing may be a big "Do!" for one child, but a huge "Never do that!" for another. How are we supposed to know what to do?

*

This book is for parents who want a way out of their endless loop of frustration. It's also for those who cannot find a way to understand their child, get through to their child, or re-establish that loving connection they felt the moment they cradled their newborn.

What if I told you that our problem as frustrated parents has less to do with *how* we parent, and more to do with *why* we parent? Let me tell you a bit about my own experience and epiphany:

Twenty-six years ago, I was a new mother with a beautiful, yet challenging baby boy, Jordan. Amid the chaos and unpredictability of that first year of his life, there were two things my then-husband Carl and I knew with certainty:

1. Jordan didn't take no for an answer.
2. Jordan never gave up.

From his first breath, our precious boy was volatile and ornery. He would thrash angrily whenever we would try to change his diaper (yes, it took a team of two), as if he were furious at being disturbed. Similarly, he would rage when I switched him to the other breast during feedings. It was clear that this was a boy who was going to fight to have things his own way. As he grew up, he had a lot to say, and was easily infuriated when we couldn't decipher what he was trying to tell us.

He seemed so uninterested in pleasing us that, at one point, I worried that he might be a sociopath. When he would construct a tower out of blocks, Carl and I might say, "Wow! Look at that great tower you've built!" Unlike other kids, he *glared* back, and in one swift motion crashed the tower to the ground. He instantly caught onto the warm fuzzies, baby talk, and hollow praises many parents are quick to award their kids, and wanted no part of it. He has always been a steadfast contrarian. The words to nighttime lullabies had to be changed: "lulla-byes" had to become "lulla-hellos," "goodnights" were to be "good mornings." As he grew, he would never buy into conventional wisdom. To this day, Jordan makes his own observations and builds his own truths before accepting anyone else's. He definitely hears his own drummer.

I had long dreamed of being a mom. I have always adored kids and spent many years as the top neighborhood babysitter, fully booked due to my great competence, enthusiasm, and deep connection with children. Motherhood would surely be even better, I imagined, with my own precious child to nurture. The reality, however, was something quite different altogether. Returning to Jordan's first year, the relentlessness of parenthood and dealing with his unpredictability were taking their toll. Between the exhaustion, post-partum hormonal imbalances, and my expectations, it was overwhelming, and I started feeling like a failure. Resentment crept in, which led to even less patience, even though more patience was needed. I felt doomed to an exhausting vicious cycle. I foresaw years of pushing and getting pushed back. But, a moment of grace changed my life forever.

How ironic that my own mother was the catalyst for this moment of grace. At the time Jordan was born, we had a decent relationship. You might say we were in a period of détente. Growing up, though, our relationship had been explosive. As a child, I felt like I couldn't do anything right, and I didn't understand why. I was smart, a hard-working student, and was well liked in school and the neighborhood. Each day, I tried to prove my worth to her, but invariably, something I said or did seemed to affect her like nails on a chalkboard. Conflicts flared at every turn. For instance, I loved wearing the latest clothing styles, but my mother was a firm believer in hand-me-downs, and I felt ashamed, believing that I was vain and superficial. When I would save up my babysitting money to buy my own clothes, she would tell me I was "frittering away" my money. At age ninety-one, she remembered and told me the story of how, at age seven, *she* had been shamed by *her* mother for wanting a brand new, beautiful gray corduroy dress. In retrospect, I wasn't the overly vain one — she thought *she* was.

To avoid rubbing her the wrong way, I did what all children do: I assumed something was wrong with me and I tried to hide whatever it was. Trying to keep myself contained was a struggle, though. I had a big personality. I was too much. Feeling so misunderstood, I would rage when she would frustrate me.

To be sure, the family circumstances around my birth were tragic and challenging. Mom was overwhelmed and depressed, having been widowed two months before I was born. She was thirty-three years old, and had three children and a newborn.

When my intense personality began to emerge as a toddler, I became a thorn in her side. I was the squeaky wheel, always making my needs and desires known. "Why can't you just be like the others?" she would ask. The question itself filled me with shame. There was something wrong with being who I was, and at that young age, I couldn't understand why or what I might do about it. Let me be clear, though: I never doubted that my mother loved me. She just didn't seem to like me very much.

Years later, as a new parent, I still carried around an indignant rage for how I felt she had treated me. With this long-standing tension simmering just below the surface, I was a worn out mother of a demanding seven-month-old baby who ended every exhausting day with a forty-five-minute rage before falling off to sleep.

> My mom was overwhelmed and depressed, having been widowed just two months before I was born.

One night, when Mom was visiting, she experienced first-hand this intense nighttime ritual. After Jordan had finally fallen asleep, we peeked into his crib. As we watched him contentedly suck his thumb, Mom smiled and whispered, "Look at him. What a sweet angel he is when he's sleeping," repeating that classic refrain of parents on their last nerve, when, at last, their child blessedly sleeps and their hearts soften.

Her comment cut me like a knife. Instead of feeling grateful that she could give my son the loving acceptance that she hadn't been able to give me, she triggered something massive in me, and I shut down. With an uncharacteristic blank stare on my face, I hissed, "No, I don't see that. Not even when he's sleeping."

Something had changed, and Mom later told me that my vacant eyes alarmed her. She blurted out, "But, Nancy, he's just like you!"

Sharp inhale.

"*What?*"

In that millisecond, I experienced a moment of grace, a profound knowing with mind, body, and heart that changed my life, my mom's life, and the lives of my children.

Instantly, in seeing Jordan as being in my shoes for the

very first time, I had the answer to the question that had been plaguing me all my life: what had I done to be treated this way? I hadn't done anything…I was just too much for her to handle. I had been feeling overwhelmed by Jordan, and I now understood that my own mother had felt the same toward me.

Did that mean Jordan would feel as I had? Would he follow in his mother's footsteps and ask himself what was wrong with him? In that moment, the idea that he could feel the kind of pain that I had felt, because of something I did, was abhorrent to me, and powerful enough to create an instant commitment to do everything in my power to prevent that from happening.

The enormity of these revelations jolted me right out of my self-righteously indignant childhood story about "the way she treated me." By stepping out of that story, I opened the door to feel compassion for my mother and what she had gone through in raising me. I could now see with sickening clarity how easy it would have been to unconsciously go down the same path as hers. Like an emergency defibrillator, these truths shocked my heart into unconditional acceptance for my feisty, determined, ferocious, and precious little boy. In that moment, I vowed I would understand and accept Jordan as he was and *never make him feel wrong for being himself.*

Twenty-six years later, I value my decision to accept Jordan's disposition, his outlook on life, and his personality one hundred percent. I had to look at it like this: Jordan was born with a feisty, strong-willed temperament. He can't help his strong feelings, and it's not his fault that he's not easygoing. Allowing him to be who he is was the first step in raising him to become the best version of himself.

The second, and equally important step became apparent

quickly. If you accept your child, you must also provide the leadership to teach your child how to be effective in the world. A child who acts like the alpha dog, running roughshod over everyone and everything in his path, will not grow up happy, healthy, or thriving. It takes a parent or caregiver to provide the guidance necessary to thrive in the family, the community, and the larger world. Parents must lead with acceptance.

My life has been the perfect storm for this work. From a sad, misunderstood, and angry child, to an accepting parent and transformed daughter, my journey has provided abundant grist for the mill.

When Jordan was three, we had another son, Ethan. Since that turning point in Jordan's room twenty-six years ago, the boys have been both the laboratories for, and the beneficiaries of, leading with acceptance.

> My life has been the perfect storm for this work. From a sad, misunderstood, and angry child, to an accepting parent and transformed daughter, my journey has provided abundant grist for the mill.

It took many years of trial and error, and deeper study and understanding of acceptance, but I knew I was on to something. I was able to heal my relationship with my mother and raise my two sons to be exactly who they are. Together, Jordan, Ethan, my mother, and I ended a toxic legacy that threatened the well-being of each of us and that of our future generations. I learned to lead with acceptance and, as I shared my philosophy and offered my techniques to family and friends, their feedback confirmed that it was powerful and sorely needed by many families. Maya Angelou once said, "As soon as healing takes place, go out and heal somebody else." Heeding her wise words, I offer leading with acceptance.

One thing I must clarify is that adopting acceptance is not the answer to every child behavior problem. There are so many variables involved in how your child sees the world, acts, or feels. I'm not claiming that any of the many behavioral or developmental issues that your family may face won't require intervention from a medical expert. Children act out for many reasons, to which many experts, teachers, and parents I have interviewed will attest. Just as every child is different, each circumstance is entirely unique.

No matter what your child may specifically be going through, however, the message of this book still stands: every child needs to consciously know that they are accepted for who they are. It is a basic premise of this book that every child who is not accepted for who they are is profoundly affected, whether they act out now or later.

Of course, it hasn't been easy. In today's world, the do's and do not's of parenting are more confusing than ever. I hope to generate conversation, raise awareness, and help guide parents to adopt a new way to view parenthood. The pressures and expectations embedded in today's society, for instance, make acceptance a difficult, at times nearly impossible, thing to embrace for many parents.

It is a basic premise of this book that every child who is not accepted for who they are is profoundly affected, whether they act out now or later.

I urge every parent to lead with acceptance. Leading with acceptance will allow you to help your children become the best version of who they are. It will allow them to live in integrity with their true selves and optimize their chances for a happy, well-adjusted life. The goal of this book is to help you renew the way you see your child — and to use these fresh eyes to redefine what it will take to ensure that your child and your relationship thrive. Isn't this what we want? Let's not lose sight of something so basic.

*

In Part I, we will discuss the power of recognizing acceptance as a basic human need and how parents can harness it to raise a healthy, well-adjusted, thriving child.

In Part II, we'll look at the specifics of how to accept the Child You've Got, including the confusing question of exactly what you should accept and shouldn't accept about your child. This is the starting point for creating a relationship that allows a child to become the best version of who they are.

Part III will show you how to be the leader you need to be while using acceptance as your starting point, as well as making the case that everyone thrives when parents lead with acceptance.

Part I:
Acceptance —
The Forgotten Human Need

Acceptance is a fundamental human need, but in modern-day parenting, we seem to have lost sight of its importance. Amid the avalanche of parenting advice and techniques available everywhere parents turn, the message seems to be on getting children to comply and behave. But children misbehave for a reason and, if they don't feel understood and accepted, no technique or chart is going to get rid of the problem. Like putting a Band-Aid on a broken leg, it's not going to be effective. We need to start focusing on the importance of acceptance in raising our children.

When acceptance is the starting point in parenting, it builds a warm, solid, connected foundation for a lifetime relationship of mutual respect. Feeling appreciated and understood for who we are puts us on the path to authentic success. We grow up comfortable in our own skin, aware of both our gifts and our challenges, and willing and able to shine our own unique light out into the world.

Sadly, the opposite is also true: not feeling seen and understood for who we are affects us at the deepest level. It leaves us wounded, concealing parts of who we are to avoid rejection and seeking approval wherever we can find it.

Chapter 1: Understanding the Power of Acceptance

"The privilege of a lifetime is being who you are."
— Joseph Campbell

In Mary Shelley's classic, *Frankenstein*, the need for acceptance is a formidable theme. The Creature yearns for love and acceptance, and his realization that he will never be accepted among humans leads him to demand, and be denied, a female counterpart from his maker, Victor. The horror that plays out results from the lack of acceptance and sense of belonging that the Creature cannot endure. The universal pain of this type of isolation is taken to a violent and gruesome conclusion.

For years, readers have agreed that, despite the book's sci-fi genre, the novel is grounded in a very real theme: the power of love and acceptance, and the lifelong damage that occurs if they are denied.

The human need for acceptance is so basic and deep that when we are denied it from the first people we seek it from — our parents — we spend a lifetime scrambling to find it wherever we can: through peers, crime, and gangs, leaving us vulnerable to predators, and at risk for dangerous escapes like self-harm and suicide.

A young man who feels that those around him genuinely respect and accept his right to his own feelings, point of view, temperament, and life goals is more likely to unearth his gifts and thrive as a confident, happy individual.

Isn't it common sense that, when a human being feels accepted from the start, she is more likely to have a secure attachment with those who accept her? Isn't she more likely to have confidence that her personality is unique and precious, or that the way she sees the world can add value to it? A young man who feels that those around him genuinely respect and accept his right to his own feelings, point of view, temperament, and life goals is more likely to unearth his gifts and thrive as a confident, happy individual. After all, why would a person who has been valued and respected his whole life want to settle for something less than what he knows he deserves?

Angie, twenty-two, from Northport, New York, says that acceptance and respect are valued in her family. Because of it, she has a strong bond with her younger brother and with her two parents, a bond that she believes will last her whole life. Although the siblings have distinct personalities (Angie is eloquent and bubbly like her mother, while her brother is brainy and reserved like her father), the four are a tight clan. Simply spending time together, she says, is a regular family activity. They all connect easily and deeply, even though they're all quite different. Since her parents prioritized being aware of and open to their children's gifts and deficits from the beginning, their family identity is strong and inclusive of everyone.

Angie's family is not just a best-case scenario. This type of connected, thriving family is possible as long as acceptance is prioritized.

Acceptance Is a Basic Human Need

Feeling accepted should not be a privilege reserved for a lucky few: it is a basic human need. Those who have not been accepted for who they are often go on to live fractured and unfulfilled lives, as we will see and explore throughout this book.

The need for belonging and acceptance has been well known to experts for years, even though many parents have failed to embrace it. In 1943, psychologist Abraham Maslow published his Hierarchy of Human Needs, a pyramid[1] that guides viewers to better understand what drives human behavior. Maslow's Hierarchy is very much in use today, especially among organizational development experts, who use it to help explain how people within companies relate to each other. Maslow believed that, once the needs on each level were met, an individual could and would progress to keep satisfaction at the next level, and the next, and so on. Those who can't get their needs met at a particular level remain there, continually attempting to satisfy the unmet needs.

At the lowest level, he listed basic physiological functions; at the next, he listed basic safety functions. At the third level, however, he incorporates the most basic *emotional* functions; once these needs are satisfied, an individual can develop better self-esteem, and the more fulfilling goal of self-actualization.

As your basic needs are met, the higher you can advance up through Maslow's pyramid, and the more capable you become of fostering and developing more aspects of yourself.

You'll see that the need to belong and be accepted is a basic emotional need coming just after the safety and physiological needs of shelter, food, and basic bodily functions.

Does this make sense to you? It seems logical that someone who develops strong self-esteem and a great sense of confidence is more likely to be open to new experiences or strive for more creative goals.

Carl Rogers, one of the founders of humanistic psychology, believed that every human being is born with a self-actualizing tendency. In Rogers' view, children need unconditional positive regard and acceptance to develop into their unique true selves. According to Rogers, the power of acceptance is so necessary that, if parents withhold it, children will naturally deny or distort the disapproved parts as a matter of survival. The saddest example of this is when children blame themselves when their parents abuse them. But children do this naturally.

On a recent walk by the riverfront in downtown Napa, I watched a nine- or ten-year-old boy interact with his young sister, who appeared to be around three. She was too small to see over the railing and watch the ducks in the river, so he picked her up and they watched, leaning against the fence together as he held her up. After a minute or so, she squirmed out of his arms and slipped down, banging her knee on the cement just as their mother walked up. The little girl burst into tears and mom immediately chastised her son for hurting his sister.

According to Carl Rogers, the power of acceptance is so necessary that, if parents withhold it, children will naturally deny or distort the disapproved parts as a matter of survival.

As his mother criticized him, I saw his face fall, as though his heart was breaking for the thousandth time. He had lifted his sister sweetly and helpfully so she could enjoy the ducks; now his mother was yelling at him for hurting her. As his mom and sister walked away, he remained at the railing with his head hung low, as if he were ashamed of himself for not realizing his mistake before it happened.

Feeling for him, I walked closer and gently said, "You like helping your sister, don't you?"

He looked up, warily.

I continued, hoping some understanding and acceptance might help. "I can see what a fine young man you are," I said. "Don't ever change that kind, helpful part of yourself. It's really neat."

His face relaxed and he smiled at me. Perhaps this simple acknowledgement of his helpful nature planted a positive seed in his psyche.

Many studies, some of which I cite throughout this book, justify that acceptance creates strong attachment. Were you fortunate enough to experience it, think back to someone in your life who really understood you, saw you for who you were, and accepted you lovingly. How did you feel about that person and how strongly attached did you feel? When I ask people this question, they invariably smile and tell me that they would have done anything for that person. Don't you want to be that person in your child's life?

My sister Jackie, the youngest of the five siblings, tells me she felt completely seen, accepted, and embraced by her piano teacher, Herma. Jackie's face lights up and she smiles as she recalls this part of her childhood. The hour a week she spent in Herma's living room studio was balm for her soul. Herma had a special way of making Jackie feel her own preciousness, and, forty years later, that unconditional acceptance remains a powerful memory for her. Just thinking about Herma brings Jackie joy.

*

This book will show that feeling accepted:

1. positively affects how we perceive ourselves, and
2. positively affects every relationship we have.

But it can be challenging to know exactly what to accept, in any relationship.

Acceptance of What?

A parent who wants to accept who their child is may have trouble identifying what should be accepted and what should not. Does accepting who someone is mean unconditional acceptance of his or her behavior? Let's be clear right up front: it does not. The distinction here is between *who someone is*, and *what someone does*. This difference is of paramount importance and is explored extensively throughout this book.

Who your child is = CoreSelf → ACCEPT

What your child does = Behavior → MANAGE

Babies are born with certain traits that remain relatively stable over their lifetimes. Sure, these traits can be tweaked, but they will not disappear or transform. Accepting who someone is means accepting the traits that we are born with that cannot be changed.

Since researchers first realized that there is a biological component to our personalities, they have been trying to identify and describe this piece we're born with. It is often called temperament, and the term encompasses our traits, quirks, way of looking at the world, and our gifts and challenges.

Babies are born with certain traits that remain relatively stable over a lifetime. Sure, these traits can be tweaked, but they will not disappear or transform.

Attempting to change someone's temperament will cause problems sooner or later. This makes even more sense if you consider how you would feel if someone decided your personality was unacceptable and tried to change it because it would make life easier for him. When I was growing up, my persistent and questioning nature did not please my mother. I remember her asking, actually almost pleading with me, "Why can't you be like the others?" As a child, I had no answer for her. I just knew that the very question shamed me deeply. I felt wrong for being who I was, but I felt powerless to be different.

Both scientists and parents can attest to the inborn nature of some traits. One man remarked that his younger brother had a distinctly peculiar way of seeing the world from the very beginning, which is exhibited in the hilarious personality he still has today.

A mother said that her daughter would meticulously organize her dresser drawers from a very young age, and her methodical nature led to her success working in government.

Another mom, Laurie, said that, in clear contrast with her own big personality, her daughter Emily was as reserved and quiet as a toddler as she is today.

Mark, a father from Sachse, Texas, said he knew from the start that his daughter was a natural leader. He explained, "When she was about six days old, the RN in charge of the maternity ward came in and told my wife that she had noticed something about Margie that she had never seen before. Keep in mind that this is a woman who had been in charge of the maternity ward for more than twenty-five years. When Margie would cry, she said, all of the babies would cry. When she stopped, they did, too. She had watched Margie for several days to see if it was just a one-time thing, but it happened every single time. She was sure that Margie was a natural born leader." Mark says that the nurse was right, and that Margie has gone on to exhibit strength and leadership skills, publishing newspaper articles at fifteen and becoming an honors pre-med student in college.

Noted parenting author and researcher Michael Gurian calls the attributes that emerge and endure from the beginning of our lives our core nature. While our life experiences have an effect on how we later react to situations, compartmentalize emotions, or make choices, his view of our innate traits is based on the latest science. I echo Gurian's idea of the core nature, and expand on it, calling it the CoreSelf. Chapter 5 will lead you through a deeper discovery of each aspect of your child's CoreSelf, and, in Chapter 7, you will be invited to learn the role that your own CoreSelf plays in your relationship with your child.

Despite widespread agreement that we're born with certain traits and that they influence our way of being for a lifetime, why is acceptance so elusive for so many of us? How is it that we have lost touch with something so basic?

Certainly, confusion over what should be accepted and what can be changed can lead to inaction. Parents don't want to create the kind of narcissists seen in reality TV or sitcoms, exemplified in the extreme by the character of "Never" in the television comedy *Louie*. Never's mother has raised him to believe that everything he does is perfect, and that he should never be asked to change anything about himself, ever. Although he is comically misguided, Never is so insufferable that he might be held up as the poster child warning against the dangers of too much acceptance.

Also, as one mother mentioned to me, there is a widespread belief that, if we put our mind to something, we have the power to change it, even if it means hoping another individual will change the essence of who they are. This mother talked about her teenage wish, that her younger brother would outgrow his tendency to become terribly flustered in large groups. Over time, however, she came to realize that, no matter how often she coached, supported, or encouraged him, he would never enjoy social gatherings the way she did. Further, he did not wish to change, because he was comfortable the way he was. What deepened their connection in the long term was accepting that he was who he was, and not trying to change him.

> ## Just because a trait remains stable over a lifetime doesn't mean it cannot be managed.

Finally, some people believe that, if you accept someone as they are, they will have no reason to grow. Underlying this objection is the unspoken belief that what motivates people to grow and improve themselves is the expectations of others. This is simply not true, as anyone who has ever tried to quit smoking or lose weight to please someone else can attest.

Fred Rogers, the man behind the character in television's *Mister Rogers' Neighborhood*, once said, "Knowing that we are loved exactly as we are gives us all the best opportunity for growing into the healthiest of people." Did anyone understand children better than Mr. Rogers? However, just because a trait remains stable over a lifetime doesn't mean it cannot be managed. In fact, it is the duty of parents to socialize their children by managing them. Good parenting is essential in order to influence the expression of CoreSelf traits.

Kim John Payne, author of *Simplicity Parenting*,[2] has described how our children's natural quirkiness can become a gift if balanced, or a disorder if stressed. This idea is discussed in Chapter 8 as we explore how parents can lead their children to become the best version of who they are. But here's a fascinating paradox: by accepting who your child is, you create the strong attachment that makes your child receptive to your influence as you guide them to positive expression of their

CoreSelf in the world.

If we can embrace the concept that the CoreSelf we're born with is our CoreSelf throughout our lives, think of how much better we will not only connect with others, but also ultimately nurture others to shine. Acceptance means finding a way to work with these innate traits, something we'll look at in the next chapter in the context of parenthood.

When We Don't Feel Accepted

Just as being accepted can create boundless confidence for an individual, not being accepted can cause problems that can take a lifetime to mend, if at all.

Not being accepted:

1. harmfully affects how we perceive ourselves, and
2. negatively affects every relationship we have.

Kathy was born adventurous and curious about the world. However, she was also born into a family of rule followers. This was a constant source of friction between her and her parents (and her and her siblings!) as she grew up. She was labeled as the bad girl, and felt misunderstood and thwarted. To this day, she carries an image of herself as a bad girl, even though she is a beloved mother, grandmother, wife, sister, daughter, and health care professional.

I asked her whether it would have been different had her parents said to her, "You are much more adventurous than we are, which is sometimes hard for us since we're not like that. But it's our job as your parents to keep you safe and develop the good judgment you'll need to be adventurous out in the world without us." I wondered whether she would have rebelled to the extent that she did.

She smiled wistfully, and said, "No, because I wouldn't have felt like such a misfit."

When we aren't seen and accepted as we are, we live in an emotionally uncomfortable state, feeling that it is wrong to be who we are. If we feel that it is wrong to be ourselves, we try to hide who we are, or at least the parts that are misunderstood or not accepted. We've all known people who suppress parts of themselves in an effort to be loved by their parents. One person may not pursue their artistic side in favor of "making a decent living." Another will become who they think they need to be to fit within their family. Annika, a woman with a lovely voice and three musical teenagers, told me about the root of her paralyzing self-consciousness about singing in front of people. She grew up in a religiously fundamentalist home and, when she was seven, she came home from Bible camp enthralled with the expressive soulfulness of one song's syncopated refrain. As she "let it all hang out" and sang it for her parents, she immediately sensed the discomfort of her strictly controlled mother and, while nothing was directly spoken, Annika knew immediately that this piece of who she was needed to be kept under wraps.

When we aren't seen and accepted as we are, we live in an emotionally uncomfortable state, feeling that it is wrong to be who we are.

When we hurt from feeling unseen and unaccepted, we gravitate toward those situations where we do feel accepted, leaving ourselves vulnerable, and easy marks for the manipulations of others. We look for external validation of our worthiness. We are needy, which can lead to a lack of discernment.

Because we don't feel our own worth, we settle for crumbs. When people don't provide us with the validation we crave, we may turn to substance abuse and other methods to numb our underlying pain. Unless we find a healing path, we will be perpetually dealing with the symptoms of the underlying wound.

Sheri, who is from Chicago but now resides in Northern California, grew up without acceptance from and a sense of belonging with her family. Although she was soothing and kind to others by nature, she did not feel like her traits were accepted as gifts, casting her on a lifelong search for her place.

"It wasn't a family in which there was much love," she said. "My brother, sister, and I were basically in competition for whatever scraps there were, and there was no bonding. We were out for ourselves. It took me five decades to say, 'I deserve more.' So, yeah, it totally determined my life and what I expected from the world. The world has never been a safe place for me. I never expected to get nurturing or understanding or support."

Sheri's one saving grace, however, was the love she received from her grandmother. "I used to sit on her lap way past the time I was supposed to, even up until I was thirteen or fourteen. If I wanted to talk, she would listen. I didn't have to be anything or do anything. That's what saved me. That's how I got love."

Sheri also explained that the absence of love and acceptance as a child has taken — and in many ways is still taking — a lot of introspection and therapy to heal. Over time, she's nurtured her natural tendency to help others, volunteering for years in homeless shelters and hospices. Ultimately, she became a doula, a birth coach for expectant moms. As she now dedicates her life to welcoming new life into the world, she says, "There's nothing more important than feeling wanted and cherished and respected. Being given the space and acknowledgment that you are a unique valuable human being is essential and, if you don't get that as a child, it's a lifelong job to find it. At least for me it's been."

> When we hurt from feeling unseen and unaccepted, we gravitate toward those situations where we do feel accepted, leaving ourselves vulnerable, and easy marks for the manipulations of others.

In the next chapter, we'll explore acceptance specifically within the context of parenting. The goal is to understand how we can prioritize acceptance as the foundation for a child to grow into a strong and thriving adult.

Chapter 2: Bringing the Power of Acceptance to Parenting

"Acceptance is like the fertile soil that permits a tiny seed to develop into the lovely flower it is capable of becoming."
— Dr. Thomas Gordon, *The Power of the Language of Acceptance*

Accepting your child should be as much of a commitment as having one in the first place. Ideally, every parent would view integrating acceptance into the day-to-day relationship with his child as basic as meeting a child's other needs, such as toilet training, teaching manners, and instilling healthy habits. Just as we discussed the powerful positive effect that acceptance has on the individual in Chapter 1, parents should also see the significance of acceptance in a child's development. Acceptance leads to secure attachment, and secure attachment leads to positive outcomes as children grow up.

Making the conscious choice to lead with acceptance lays a powerful foundation for thriving children and lifelong healthy relationships.

My Job as a Parent

Does this sound familiar?

> "*My job as a parent is to raise a child who is a success, and I have the wisdom, experience, and judgment to know what it means to be a success. I help shape and mold my child to follow this path, and when he complies with my expectations, he earns my acceptance and approval. When he doesn't comply, we battle, and I look for new ways to keep him on the path to success. Repeat as necessary.*"

Of course, we want success for our children. Isn't it our job as parents to raise children who succeed? But let's look at how we define success here. In this all too common view, the parent is the one who decides what is meant by success. After all, parents possess the wisdom, experience, and judgment to understand what it means to be successful and what it takes to get there.

But what really happens when parents decide what success is? Our job then becomes to mold, shape, cajole, and push our children to satisfy our idea of what it takes to be, or become, successful. In this model, we accept our children conditionally, when they satisfy our idea of how they should act, or of what's best for them, by following the path that we feel is best. We've set things up so that our children must stay on the success track that we've defined for them, and constantly meet benchmarks to gain our acceptance and approval.

But what about focusing on your particular child's needs, and accepting who she is at her core?

Jeanette, a mother and writer living in Milwaukee, shared her perspective on how goals of success can naturally tie into parenting: "Part of it is that you don't want your kids to suffer failure or go through the things that you suffered through as a kid. You want things to be better for them."

As parents, we have that natural sense that we *should* know what's best. We understand that the world is an uncertain and sometimes scary place. We *should* be guiding our children toward certain benchmarks along the path toward success, shouldn't we? Isn't it our job? The best-intentioned parents simply want their children to have the greatest chance for a successful, happy life, and, as you read on, you'll discover the stories of many parents who genuinely want the best for their children. As the saying goes, if we push them to shoot for the moon, the greater the chance they'll land among the stars. What parents don't wish this for their child?

The pressures of academic success have permeated today's homes. Many parents believe that bright futures are within the reach of only the top students from top schools, or kids who are most prepared to excel in the workplace. It all fuels a value system based on how many achievements their child can accumulate, as if preparing your child for success is equal to raising her right. A loving parent truly wants what's best for her child; perhaps it's the fear that she won't rear her son or daughter to live independently in the world that drives her to follow these dictums.

Ask any child who failed to live up to his parents' idea of success, and you'll likely hear that they never felt good enough, or that their parents had expectations that they could not live up to.

Experts say that what has resulted is a generation of parents attempting to raise superadults by molding their children into über-capable beings. And how do they do this? It requires controlling every detail of the child's life in order to keep them on course for maximum success. As explored in the book *The Overachievers: The Secret Lives of Driven Kids* by Alexandra Robbins, there are many negative consequences when children live with this relentless pressure to achieve. "Overachiever culture is disturbing not because it exists but because it has become a way of life. Nationwide, the relentless pursuit of perceived perfectionism has spiraled into a perpetual cycle of increasing intensity and narrowing ideals."[3] In her most recent work, *Teach Your Children Well: Parenting for Authentic Success*, Madeline Levine wrote, "Every measure of child and adolescent mental health has deteriorated since we've decided that children are best served by being relentlessly pushed, overloaded, and tested. Our current version of success is a failure."[4]

Who is paying the price for our misguided ideas? Certainly our children are. Ask any child who failed to live up to his parents' idea of success, and you'll likely hear that they never felt good enough, or that their parents had expectations that they could not live up to. Why? Because their parents' expectations had nothing to do with who they were, and everything to do with who the parents were.

As if that's not damaging enough (both to the child's self-worth and the parent/child relationship), here's the double whammy: when acceptance is conditional on a child's actions, he is unlikely to develop the warm and secure attachment that develops when acceptance is given unconditionally. Without that positive attachment, many of these children don't even want to please their parents. Even if they were capable of living up to their parents' expectations, they refuse to do so. They don't feel seen, understood, or accepted for who they are, and once they reach a certain age, they just stop trying.

Parents are paying a toll for these misguided ideas as well. Remember the hamster wheel? If you continue to parent under this old model, don't be surprised to find yourself going in circles, with the same problems popping up over and over again. Don't be surprised to find yourself back at square one, constantly seeking a solution to the same (albeit bigger and bigger) problem. And don't be surprised when the new "fix" fails to solve the problem, because if your child does not feel seen and accepted for who he is, attempting to change his behavior without addressing the underlying issue will not work in the long term.

Around age twelve, I would sometimes become so enraged with my mother that I would grab her forearms and try to dig my nails into her flesh until I drew blood. In my fury, there was something intensely satisfying about wounding her in this way. I was punished for this behavior, and I was always remorseful and ashamed of it, but it was bound to recur because we did not deal with the underlying issue that was driving my rage: that I felt painfully unseen and misunderstood.

There is a common misconception that if a parent accepts who a child is, they won't ever strive to improve in any way. For example, some parents I know assume that if you don't challenge a child from the start, she won't be able to discipline herself as an adult. Another fear is that, if a parent finds her child's temperament different and puzzling, the child will have a hard time interacting with others later. In theory, these may sound like good ideas. But, in many cases, this idea of molding them for the better is simply not working. Levine calls this "helicopter parenting" and has a message for these parents: You are not helping your kids, and it doesn't have to be this way.

Robert Frick, PhD, has written about the paradoxical idea that a firm hand creates strong people. He dispels the notion that if you, the parent, don't push your children, they will not want to grow. He says, "Children want to grow. They want to be stronger, more competent, more adult. So, you do not need to push them to grow. Instead, you can accept your children." He continues: "What do children really need to grow? Love. Acceptance. Someone to support them, encourage them, root for them, be with them when they succeed and when they fail…"[5]

As Frick insists, kids don't need someone telling them their faults and how they should change. Take another look at the self-actualization pyramid of Maslow's ideas that I introduced earlier. Notice that it stresses that human beings have an innate desire to grow, and to ultimately attain all of their physiological, emotional, and spiritual needs. Yet, without a strong foundation based on acceptance, it's a lifelong struggle to move up the pyramid. Accept your child, encourage your child, support your child.

After all, in raising your child, you are building him up to live and prosper independently from you in the future. As one mom interviewed for this book put it: "The relationship between parent and child is the only one whose goal is separation and not closeness."

Too often, parents see their child's degree of success in the world as a reflection of their character or abilities as a parent.

It also goes beyond the culture of success. Jennifer Little, PhD, an expert in special education and psychology, remarked, "The biggest problem I've seen is that parents have an ego-interest in the children, to be seen and not heard, be the "winner" or top of the class, be the star athlete or prom princess…as a way to validate the parents themselves. The parent measures his/her worth as a person and as a parent by the vague and unrealistic standards and goals of achievement that they force a child to attain."

Jennifer brings up a powerful point: so often, parents see their child's degree of success in the world as a reflection of their character or abilities as parents.

In sharing the insights she's gathered about parenting throughout her career, Jennifer also shared her own upbringing: "In my job as a special educator, I identified all too well with my students," she wrote to me. "Growing up, I was constantly mourning the fantasy mother I never experienced: the mother who wanted me, who loved me (showing and telling me she did), who respected me (not putting me down or making me feel inferior to others), who cared about me and who wanted the best for me… I came to believe that I was not good enough, that I wasn't a wanted child, and that no matter what I ever did or didn't do I could never get my parents' approval or acceptance." She added, "It took me a very long time (many decades of focused and intentional work) to work through the psychological damage that resulted from my upbringing."

What Jennifer brings up touched me deeply: that not being accepted while growing up can leave a painful mark, or lead to years of "mourning." It's unfair. As we grow up and continue to hide the unaccepted pieces of who we are from the world, we hide them from ourselves as well. Eventually, we come close to losing touch with these parts of ourselves. We live inauthentic lives and we may be prevented from ever feeling positively connected with this person we are meant to be so close with: our parent.

The Paradox of Raising a Child in Your Vision

Amid the louder demands that your child's value is in how successful he is, we've neglected the true priority: first encouraging your child to shine in his own skin. *That* — not conditional benchmarks of achievement — is the foundation upon which strong adults emerge.

Look around you at people who might have been rejected as children. Ask yourself whether they are healthy, positive people, or people who might have been shattered by their upbringings.

Encouraging your child to shine in his own skin — not conditional benchmarks of achievement — is the foundation upon which strong adults emerge.

Amy, a social worker living in Rockville, Maryland, often sees parents overeager to mold their children in ways *they* deem appropriate. "First, parents want the perfect child. They want the best, smartest, happiest kid in school and one that is going to be successful in the future but they don't always realize that even the most successful people are definitely not perfect," Amy says. "Parents don't realize the repercussions of doing this."

It's time to put acceptance front and center as the first item of business on every parent's checklist.

Benefits of Acceptance in Child-Rearing:

1. The love between parent and child is solidified. In *Between Parent and Child*, Dr. Haim Ginott writes, "When children feel understood, their loneliness and hurt diminish. When children are understood, their love for the parent is deepened."[6]

2. The child is more likely to develop positive outcomes later in life.[7] We feel worthwhile because our parents like who we are, apart from what we achieve. We can be ourselves, because we're comfortable with who we are, or comfortable in our own skin. We have no reason to hide or feel ashamed of parts of ourselves. As one psychotherapist explained to me, "Your children are fully formed souls that are worthy of respect, acceptance, support. If you don't give them that, there's a whole lot of trouble that can occur."

Being accepted allows us to have a realistic view of ourselves, not needing to distort or hide pieces of who we are. This gives us the best opportunity to be happy and free in the deepest parts of ourselves. I call this being given *license to shine*. When someone truly shines, she's better equipped not only to explore and develop her own identity, but also to positively affect the lives of those around her.

1. Kids who have open and accepting relationships with their parents have the best chance of making better choices in both today's and tomorrow's worlds. According to a recent study, teenagers who often eat dinner with their families are likelier to say that their parents know more about their day to day lives. And this knowledge and connection between parent and child is linked to decreased usage of marijuana, alcohol, and tobacco.[8]

2. The stronger your relationship with your child is, the greater chance you have that your child will look to you for guidance, rather than reject you as overly controlling. Dr. Thomas Gordon, the author of this chapter's beautiful introductory quote, also stated, "The inevitable result of consistently employing power to control [your] kids when they are young is that [you] never learn how to *influence*."[9]

The power of acceptance can create lasting love, and leading with acceptance will get you started — or restarted — down this win/win path.

You are raising your child to shine in *her* future, not to subscribe to the life goals *you* may value.

Acceptance Should Not Be Conditional

Our goal of raising children who are successful hasn't changed, but we must adjust our definition of success to honor the child we've got. As we explored in Chapter 1, each individual is born with a unique core nature. You are raising your child to shine in *her* future, not to subscribe to the life goals *you* may value.

Here's the new model for success:

"My job as a parent is to help my child become a success by becoming the best version of who he is. My first task is to understand and accept who he is. While accepting and honoring who he is, I lead our family so he learns the values and the proper behavior in our family, our community, and the world. I do not impose my idea of success on him; instead, by accepting who he is, I help him get to know himself and become comfortable in his

own skin. In this way, I help ensure his lifelong well-being as he becomes the best version of who he is."

When you raise your children to become the best version of who they are, you ensure their lifelong well-being, and give them license to shine.

What Is License to Shine?

Marianne Williamson wrote, "I am meant to shine, as children do. I was born to make manifest the glory of God that is within me."[10]

When children feel accepted, they are given *license to shine.* They know deeply that it is okay to be who they are. They are comfortable in their own skin. They have no reason to hide or feel ashamed of parts of themselves. They have a clear sense of what makes them happy and what does not.

Any accomplishment can be hollow to a child if she never had her heart in it from the start, as can be the case when children are pressured to achieve.

People who have been given license to shine are willing to take reasonable risks in life, since their worthiness is not tied up in accomplishments. These people tend to have a realistic view of both their challenges and their opportunities. They have a healthy foundation and are more apt to grow.

There is a difference between shining and accomplishing: any accomplishment can be hollow to a child if she never had her heart in it from the start, as can be the case when children are pressured to achieve. In contrast, when a child shines, she taps into her inner light and brings forth something from deep within. When we shine, we come alive! We will explore our inner light in Chapter 5, as an element of our CoreSelf.

I did not shine as a child. It took me many years to find my light and to shine it. Don't get me wrong, I accomplished a great deal. I was smart in school — whip-smart, actually. I skipped second grade and was still at the head of my class. A good all-around athlete, I won running races and received many shiny, blue, satin first-place ribbons. When teams were chosen on the playground, I was in the top tier. In junior high and high school, I was a cheerleader and on the honor roll. I never lacked for friends.

Accomplishing will take you far, and I did go far. By the age of twenty-four, I had graduated from Boalt Hall, an elite law school, passed the California Bar exam, and was working toward adding CPA to my sparkling credentials.

But, I discovered that it wasn't me who was sparkling, it was my résumé. I didn't shine — at least, not the way Marianne Williamson describes it. I knew what some of my strengths were, and that being smart and quick could get me far. I was good at my work. But did it bring me joy? No. Was I sharing my gifts with the world? No. Then again, at that point, I didn't have a clue what would bring me joy or what my true gifts were.

Apart from my considerable achievements, I had no real sense of who I was. At that time in my life, the notion that I even had an inner light would have been foreign to me. It would take motherhood and substantial personal growth work to uncover my capacity to shine.

As my life demonstrates, it's possible (and common!) to be quite accomplished, but not to shine. A compliant child may get all A's, take advanced placement classes and have her choice of Ivy League colleges to attend. But if her achievement is motivated by her desire to fulfill her parents' expectations, is she shining *her* light? Often, these teens burn out by the time they get to college, at the very moment they desperately need some understanding of who they are and what makes them come alive, apart from their parents' expectations.

The reverse is possible too: silently shining without outer, measurable accomplishments. A quiet, introspective child who enjoys daydreaming may shine as he passes time alone with his thoughts. To a parent focused on achievement, this can seem a complete waste of time. "Get your head out of the clouds and pay attention!" the parent might scold. Feeling criticized rather than valued discourages this type of child from pursuing his unique gifts.

> When you accept your child in a way that encourages her to beam with this authentic, realistic, and powerful sense of self-confidence, your child will be more accepting of *your* feelings, *your* wishes, and *your* point of view, too.

Another child might be restless and unproductive in the classroom, but completely at home in nature. By tapping into the wisdom of this non-academic realm, she shines.

Both these youngsters are becoming acquainted with who they truly are — tuning in and connecting on deeper levels, their gifts waiting to be uncovered. If their parents focus only on their own idea of achievement, they won't understand and accept who their children are.

As Joseph Campbell, author of *The Power of Myth*, notes,

"Your sacred space is where you can find yourself again and again."[11] A child's light and her true self is found in sacred spaces wherever they are. In the words of Hermann Hesse: "...within you there is a stillness and a sanctuary to which you can retreat at any time and be yourself..."[12] In Chapter 4, we'll delve deeper into your path to ensure your child has license to shine. It's a process, and it involves truly getting to know the child you have right in front of you. You may be astonished at the win/win this creates. When you accept your child in a way that encourages her to beam with this authentic, realistic, and powerful sense of self-confidence, your child will be more accepting of *your* feelings, *your* wishes, and *your* point of view, too. She'll be willing to listen to your opinion. She'll be more likely to cooperate with your wishes, instead of being motivated to behave based on some external benefit, like avoiding punishment or earning allowance.

Magician and mentalist Kevin Viner is a living example of the lifetime of strength, confidence, and love that being raised with acceptance brings. Now an entertainer for mainly corporate events, Kevin was enchanted with magic from an early age. "I just loved it," he said. "Magic really bridges that gap between left brain and right brain. You get to be creative, but you also have to analyze what it takes to make a trick happen." He recalled he was always a strong student. He was also determined, once performing magic at a birthday party at age eleven, despite running a 103-degree fever.

One issue arose, however, when he considered magic a career, and not just a hobby, as his parents preferred. "The thing is, my dad was always a strict parent," Kevin shared. "There was always a ton of love in the household, but I knew that if I did something wrong there would be a consequence, and if I did something right there would be a reward. I knew what was coming with any decision."

Kevin explained that, even though his dad may not have been actively fueling his son's passion, he still found ways to be supportive: "My relationship with my dad was always really good. I think, even unrelated to the magic, he was always going to do what he felt was in my best interests. There did come points where things would come up, though." When Kevin was fifteen, he got a gig doing magic at his local TGI Fridays. "I ended up getting a job doing magic from table to table, but I didn't have a car, so my dad drove me." When it came down to helping Kevin live his dream, his dad was always on board.

"College rolled around and, for a while, I really contemplated not going. The way my dad looked at it — and I understand the reason why he looked at it this way — is that he always wanted a fallback plan. That never made much sense to me, because to me it was like, 'There's no way it's not going to work.'"

> When we don't actively encourage our kids to shine, it's like cutting off the air to a precious flame.

Yet, Kevin respected his dad's advice, and today he's thankful he followed it. Because of the respectful relationship he had with his dad from the beginning, he was able to follow a path to where he is truly happy: he majored in mathematics at UC Irvine *and* established a career as a magician. Now, he can fuse the best of both worlds: he incorporates a lot of math into his show, allowing him to better connect with brainier audiences and also develop an exclusive niche in the magic world. He says that, without the acceptance his father showed him, he might never have gone down this path.

In his book *Happiness Now*, Robert Holden says that, the more self-acceptance you have, the more happiness you'll allow yourself in life. It's our job as parents to show our children how to ensure this for their future.[13]

When we don't actively encourage our kids to shine, it's like cutting off the air to a precious flame. How many children fail to pursue their passions, dreams, or their gifts because their parents did not accept certain aspects of them? Think about it: What if Hillary Rodham Clinton's parents tried to silence her from speaking her mind, or did not accept her choice to become a lawyer? What if Einstein's parents refused to recognize their young son's gifts, or had not accepted the way he viewed the world? What ambitions have your parents quieted in you?

Reminder: It's Not an Unconditional Acceptance of Behavior

I'm *not*, however, advocating for the unconditional acceptance of everything a child *does*. I'm not encouraging parents to consider a child's disrespect or engaging in dangerous activity as expressing his CoreSelf. Unfortunately, "acceptance" has become a buzzword for abdicating parental responsibility, or not teaching children proper behavior.

On the contrary, acceptance doesn't mean parents get to resign from being an authority figure, an anchor, or a leader. It doesn't mean being a friend to your child before being a parent. This is the polar opposite of being a parent who *leads* with acceptance, which means accepting who your child is, and guiding what your child does. We'll return to this concept later in this book.

The Risk of Not Making Acceptance Priority No. 1

While any child will gladly welcome the accepting, respectful connection in her relationship with her parents, she will also view parents who are dissatisfied with her as critical boss figures, not fellow human beings whom she would enjoy spending time with and including in her life. After all, would you choose to be around someone who constantly corrects you? Neither would your child.

Look at the impact on children when they feel accepted versus when they do not feel accepted:

Accepted	Not Accepted
I embrace all facets of who I am	I tuck away shameful pieces of myself/have feelings of inferiority
I feel worthwhile because my parents like me	I feel wrong for being who I am/ judge myself harshly
I don't need to be who I'm not	I try to be what my parents want me to be — I'm inauthentic
I have loyalty to and affection for my parents	I don't like my parents
I want to please my parents	I don't care about pleasing my parents
I go to my parents for advice	I don't listen to my parents
I enjoy being around my parents	I don't like being around people who correct me and don't appreciate me
I can accept my parent's strengths	I don't see the good in my parents
I consider adopting my parents' values	I reject my parents' values
I feel close to my siblings	I resent my siblings because I'm always being compared to them
I have a healthy need for significance, which I satisfy by working toward goals	I try to prove my own importance by boasting and attention-seeking
I feel worthy; I attract others who agree	I feel unworthy and settle for crumbs

Love Is Not Enough

If you're a parent reading this book, it's safe to assume you love your child. But what does that *mean*? Love itself is hard to define — centuries of poetry can attest to that. Parental love is also hard to pinpoint; people toss this term around, but when you ask them what they mean, the most specific definition many come up with is something along the lines of "the love of a parent for a child." And what looks and feels like love to one parent may be way off the mark for another.

> To accept someone means to care enough to see and understand that person, and to let them be who they are.

And yet, when we raise our kids, we do and say all kinds of things "out of love." When psychoanalyst Alice Miller says that "the mother often loves her child passionately, but not in the way he needs to be loved,"[14] she is alluding to this ambiguity about love. I wonder if, for some parents, doing things in the name of love has become an excuse for focusing on their own needs rather than the best interests of the child. Acceptance, on the other hand, is never about the parents' needs, is it? To accept someone means to care enough to see and understand that person, and to let them be who they are.

In these past two chapters, we've laid out the case for parenting by leading with acceptance. Before we jump into the specific how-to's, however, we need to deal with the elephant in the room: the Child You Want.

Reflections:

List the things your child is good at. When he does these things, is he accomplishing or *shining?*

_____

_____

_____

_____

_____

_____

_____

_____

_____

List the things your child enjoys doing that you may not consider as accomplishing anything. Does he *shine* when he does these things?

_____

_____

_____

_____

_____

_____

_____

_____

_____

Chapter 3: Letting Go of the Child You Want

"When there's an elephant in the room, name it."
— Randy Pausch, author of *The Last Lecture*

The reason you may not accept the Child You've Got might be the Child You Want. It's the elephant in the room. No one is talking about it, but it's there. You've got to look at it, understand it, and let it go. Until you do, you'll be stuck in your relationship with the Child You've Got.

The Child You Want Is Your Fantasy

At one point or another, every parent has fantasized about their ideal child. Granted, each parent differs in the degree to which they let their ideal child dictate their view of and their relationship with their child. The Child You Want may be a vague concept or someone very specific whom the parent regularly compares to their real-life child.

Parenting expert, author, and *Psychology Today* blogger Susan Newman, PhD, explains that, as we prepare for the birth of a child, we begin to connect with the baby we imagine.

As Dr. Newman explains, "That fantasy starts when the baby's in the womb. It really gels at the point at which, for example, you have a very active baby, and the father touches your stomach and says, 'We're going to have a football player!' or the baby's kind of quiet and one of the parents says, 'An intellectual, just like me!'" It's akin to romanticizing the precious moments you and the baby will have in its new nursery, or anticipating your child's first words. The fantasy of rocking or soothing a baby can actually create neural pathways and hormonal changes in the mother.

It also serves a biological purpose: The survival of the human species depends on strong parent-child attachment, most notably the bond between mother and child, which ensures proper fetal development. Although this intense connection may cause unanticipated stress, Dr. Newman points out that, "We envision happy, healthy babies and a happy home life, and we all want the best for our children. This glorification of parenthood gives us energy, and it fuels our motivation as a parent. But, when something goes awry or isn't what you thought it would be, a parent may be disappointed. Later, if your child doesn't hit a so-called 'milestone,' some parents wonder what happened to their imagined child or their dream of what parenthood would be like."

Imagining the Child You Want is normal for any parent. The Child You Want may be someone who is successful, not someone who may be inclined to live with you until he's thirty. On the other hand, you may be someone who craves this type of intense bond with your child. If you're the type of parent who yearns to truly bond with your child, the Child You Want may share your passions or have an outgoing personality like yours. It may be someone who, unlike you, never has problems with shyness and becomes the powerful woman you never had the courage to be. The Child You Want may be an athlete or a humanitarian. She may be someone nearly identical to you, who gives you the sense that there is someone else just like you in the world.

Whatever the Child You Want looks or acts like, each has one thing in common: It's a fantasy. Let me repeat that. The Child You Want is a fantasy. You have dreamt up this child to fill your needs.

The Child You Want never creates conflict and always bolsters your self-esteem. After all, when you have an ideal child, *you* are an ideal parent, living in perfect harmony.

Since the Child You Want is designed to meet your needs, the Child You Want always behaves. The Child You Want always listens to you and always agrees with you. The Child You Want never creates conflict and always bolsters your self-esteem. After all, when you have an ideal child, *you* are an ideal parent, living in perfect harmony. Maybe the Child You Want soothes the wounds from your own childhood, filling emptiness with love. The Child You Want doesn't trigger anxiety, or dark or difficult feelings. The Child You Want never pushes your buttons or questions your authority. The Child You Want fulfills the expectations that would make a parent beam with pride. Or, the Child You Want is so capable and wonderful that he banishes stress or worry from a parent's life. After all, parenting is taxing; what parent wouldn't welcome the peace of mind of a child who has no problems? Have you ever thought to yourself, "If only…"

The Child You've Got Is Real

Every parent readily admits that raising children is hard work. Unlike the Child You Want, who always makes you feel great about yourself, the Child You've Got will invariably make you question your abilities as a parent. For some parents, this doubt is akin to questioning an identity where their self-worth is tied up in being a perfect parent. Anything that doesn't support the idea that they are ideal parents is an attack on them personally. In *The Parents We Mean to Be*, author Richard Weissbourd writes, "These parents...often feel that they are doing everything for their children...and precisely because they are doing so much — because a great deal of their self-esteem is wrapped up in parenting — the stakes of failing as a parent are very high. For some of these parents, any sign of parenting failure, any expression of distress, anger, doubt, or weakness in a child, is an attack on their fundamental sense of competence."[15]

Unlike the Child You Want, who always makes you feel great about yourself, the Child You've Got will invariably make you question your abilities as a parent.

These difficult moments that are inherent in the parenting experience can push many parents to depend on their fantasy of the child they want. It's natural to hope that parenting will get easier, which is all the more reason to hope their child will become the Child They Want.

However, this tendency to sit and wait for the Child You Want to emerge can be dangerous; it's an excuse to ignore a child's true nature and hope she will become something else. Besides being a fantasy, this perfect child can also wreak havoc in your relationship with the Child You've Got. While you're fantasizing about the perfect child, your child is sitting there, completely aware that she isn't living up to this fantasy you've created. Children are much more perceptive than adults sometimes realize; he *knows* he's messing up by not being as proactive as he should, and she *knows* she's never going to be smart enough to satisfy you. Parents cannot eliminate what they don't accept, and they waste energy and create bad blood by trying to do so. As a result, rejected children leave home as soon as they can, or remain enmeshed in the tension of never being good enough for their parents.

Reality check: The Child You Want is not real. It is not hiding inside of the Child You've Got. You need to accept this fact just as much as you need to accept the child before you. It's time to let go of the Child You Want.

The Dangers of Molding the Child You've Got

Jerry, a longtime teacher who has taught in schools around the world, shared a story of one of his middle school students in Japan. She was truly brilliant and excelled in every subject. Although she was a timid, painfully shy girl (she couldn't bear to stand in front of others during class presentations, and would hide while handmade puppets spoke for her), she was at the top of her class.

Jerry recalled one parent-teacher meeting where the girl's father brought his daughter's report card to their attention. Instead of beaming, he was enraged; his daughter had straight A's, except for a B in Japanese. "I first wondered if the dad was mad because we didn't offer anything more challenging for his daughter," Jerry explained. "But soon in the conversation I knew he was angered because the grade was so low.

"He ended by saying, 'Of course, this is her least important class in our mind, but we must not let her lower her expectations.' *Her* expectations were clearly not the issue."

The girl, who perhaps had been too shy to participate enough in that class, hung her head in shame. "'We just can't have this,' the father said. Everyone was like, 'Really? Oh, that's why she's afraid of people,'" Jerry recalled, remembering how the girl before him shrank under the weight of failure.

Even though this girl was naturally bright and talented, her father had forced her into a rigid mold of perfectionism that entirely clouded how she perceived herself. "I don't know what's become of her," Jerry shared. "I don't know if she's gotten around to accepting that she is brilliant and it's okay. She just couldn't get around to being accepted by her dad, I think."

While this is a blatant example of a parent teaching a child that her value is based on fulfilling conditional benchmarks like grades, there are so many cases where parents intentionally or unintentionally try to fit their child into a mold of who they want them to be.

I've spoken to many parents who continue to hope their child will change; in almost every case, they wish for changes in ways that just can't happen. One mother was upset by her daughter's relentless energy and chattiness, which constantly got her into trouble at school. Frustrated, she often told her daughter she wished she could find a way to eventually "learn to keep her mouth shut," without stopping to consider any value in her daughter's knack for engaging others. One father hoped that his son would stop fiddling with computers and start doing his homework, without reflecting that his son's passion should be nurtured. One outgoing mother hoped that her withdrawn son was just going through a phase.

It may be clearer to outsiders that, in cases like these, there exists a fundamental misunderstanding between parent and child. I found myself asking, "How can you think that your child will be happy following in your footsteps as a lawyer when he clearly wants to be an auto mechanic?" or "Why are you pushing your teenager into social situations when you know it riddles her with anxiety?"

Have you ever wondered what would happen if a parent *never* stepped back and freed their child from the mold that they've shaped for him?

Shari Goldsmith, a life coach and therapist from Cincinnati, works with many career women. Her goal? Empowerment.

"I watched some exceptional students do all the right things, get good grades, follow their parents' expectations of what success is, and now they're lost," Shari says, adding, "They are unsure of where to go from here, because, I believe, they don't have a good sense of who they are and what they need. Possibly, their parents made too many decisions for them...." Shari's coaching highlights the value in knowing yourself, especially with clients who have come to value themselves solely in terms of their accomplishments. "I think that's a recurring theme with a lot of women," Shari explained. "A lot of women we see at being successful at their career, it's never enough. They never feel that it's truly who they are."

Sure, the Child You've Got may be primed
to act like the Child You Want.
But will that ensure her well-being?

When asked why her clients are so wrapped up in these ideas of perfectionism and success, Shari points to the culture that reared them — and may have prepared them in ways that weren't as important as they seemed. "Success is so much of getting the A, getting good grades and playing sports, and getting that scholarship in sports. All of these things are expected of young people today. I see a lot of people with young kids and there are many, many programs that they have their kids in," Shari commented, adding that her clients are people who came to depend on the mold their parents, schools, or communities have imposed. "Along the way, the kids don't get to figure out who they really are. They go through and do all the things they're supposed to do, they get the scholarships, they excel, and then they get out in the real world. I connect with a lot of young women, and we kind of forget that, when they get out there, there are different skills that they need that they don't get in school."

When asked what might be prioritized instead, Shari added, "Being successful is being able to be flexible in the workplace, being able to see outside of the box, being able to move from one project to the next, being able to take criticism, being able to interact with people, and knowing how to navigate with people. Those are the skills that really make you successful."

Shari's story begs the question: Why are some parents so adamant about molding their children to their own idea of success, when there are so many pitfalls in this rigidity? Sure, the Child You've Got may be primed to act like the Child You Want. But will that ensure her well-being?

Hillary Wollin, director of Parents-Central, a childbirth and parent support resource center in the San Francisco Bay Area, reflected on the values her own parents encouraged during her childhood. "They let us make our choices, but they had to be *their* choices," Hillary said, explaining that she only felt completely accepted if she acted according to her parents' plans. This mindset has affected her passions today. After working with many different families and children, Hillary stresses something different from the philosophies of her parents' generation: "These are little people. They have their own minds and their own opinions." This philosophy, she said, has also carried over to her relationships with her own kids. She attests that making sure her children know they are not expected to be a certain way has had immensely positive results. "My children come to me," she shared. "They can tell me anything. They know that I love them for who they are. They are not me, they are not my husband. I am pleased that they have their own set of likes, desires, and aspirations. Although they may differ from me at times, they have their own paths to follow."

As Wendy Mogel said, in *The Blessing of a Skinned Knee*, "Your child is not your masterpiece."[16] It is okay to have dreams for your child, but it's not okay when they're about you instead of her.

The Hamster Wheel: Hoping for the Child You Want

In speaking to adults whose parents never let go of the child they wanted, it's clear that they, too, get stuck on the old hamster wheel.

Sheri, the doula whom we spoke to earlier, in Chapter 1, described the emotional toll that not having been accepted by her parents took on her from a very young age. "I knew from the time I was very, very young that something wasn't right. In all the old pictures of me, I had Band-Aids on to attempt to heal the pain I felt inside. I was hurting, but I didn't know why." When she was seven or eight, she would scour the aisles of her local library's psychology section. "I knew something was wrong," she said. "And of course, I assumed it was me." After decades of emotional and spiritual healing work, Sheri finally came to accept the fact that the problem wasn't her. Now in her sixties, she's finally able to forgive her parents and has learned to give herself the acceptance she didn't receive from them.

Svea, a mom of two living in Wellesley, Massachusetts, shared her experience acting as houseparent at a prestigious all-girls boarding school. "These kids were so hungry for somebody to just love them for who they were," Svea recalled, of her years seeing girls come and go. "Parents would drop them off in limos and leave. These kids needed something different. They needed somebody to tell them, 'You're a great kid.'" Over the years, Svea has learned how crucial this support is during a child's formative years. She explains, "I saw how important it is to have another adult in a child's life, regardless of how rich or poor, to be there to give her confidence, to make her feel okay about herself, and to accept her for who she is. It's profound."

Reflections:

Can you remember your fantasies of parenthood before your children were born? How different are they from your parenting reality?

Part II:
The Parents' Path to Acceptance

As parents, it is our responsibility to meet the essential needs of our children. In the previous chapters, we've explored acceptance as one essential human need missing from many parent-child relationships.

Now, in Part II, we'll look at the specifics of how to accept the Child You've Got, including the confusing question of exactly what you should and shouldn't accept about your child. This is the starting point for creating a relationship that allows children to become the best version of who they are.

A basic tenet of leading with acceptance is that parents must distinguish between:

- who your child is and the parts you cannot change — or, the *CoreSelf*— and
- what your child does and the things you can (and must) influence — your child's *behavior*.

In Chapter 4, we will lay the groundwork for ascertaining your child's unique CoreSelf by widening your perspective of the child before you, as we ask "Who *Is* This Child?" In Chapter 5, we'll learn which parts of the child make up the CoreSelf.

In Chapter 6, we'll put this paradigm to the test, and look at common sources of conflict between parents and kids, separating out what relates to who the child is from what the child does. Then, in Chapter 7, we'll look at "hotspots," the particularly difficult areas for you as a parent to accept.

Chapter 4: Starting with the Child You've Got

"Letting go of your ideal picture may be one of the most difficult tasks you'll face as a parent but it's a necessary task. Your child needs you to do it. Holding on to what isn't real keeps you stuck."
— Stanley Turecki, *The Difficult Child*

Before you are in position to understand which things about your child should be accepted, you need as full a picture of the Child You've Got as possible. Can you expand your view of your child by asking yourself, "Who is this child?" As Wendy Mogel said, in *The Blessing of a B Minus*, try to see your child's "splendid uniqueness."[17]

Take Your Blinders Off

"How well do you know your child?" is a question I've asked many parents. As you'd imagine, they often respond, "What kind of question is that? Of *course* I know my child! I know him better than anyone." The notion that they might not know their child fully can be unsettling. But my question is not meant to offend, but rather to help parents shake up their thinking a bit.

Would you be surprised to know that being your child's parent can actually *limit* your view, instead of giving you ultimate knowledge of everything about him?

As the Buddhist teacher, nun, and author Pema Chodron once said, "The truth you believe and cling to makes you unavailable to hear anything new."[18]

As parents, we create stories about our children. As we explored in Chapter 3, the story may begin long before the child is born, and will continue evolving throughout her life. The story comes out of our perception of who our child is, based on reality, but heavily influenced by our beliefs about ourselves and the world. The story we're creating then becomes our reality, and our perspective narrows. On top of this, our interactions with our child continue to shape how we view our child's overall identity. As explained in Chapter 1, people stop showing the parts of themselves that have been rejected, trying to tuck away these traits in order to survive. Your child may show less and less of himself as time goes on.

As we explore the concept that there are things we just don't see about our children, lo and behold, there's another elephant in the room — this time in a fable about an elephant and three blind men living out in the countryside.

One day, a visitor told three blind men that there was an elephant in the village. The men had no idea what an elephant was. Mystified, they went to find out. Upon reaching the town square where the elephant was standing, a villager guided the men to feel this strange, exotic creature. Outstretching their hands, each man touched a different spot on the elephant's body as he investigated the nature of this new animal. Later, they got together to discuss what they had learned.

The first blind man, who had touched the elephant's leg,

confidently declared, "The elephant is like a pillar!"

"No, no," denounced the second blind man, who had touched the tail. "The elephant is like a rope!"

"You're both wrong," corrected the third man, who had touched the ear. "The elephant is like a big hand fan!"

A huge argument ensued, and while each man was unshakable in what he had experienced, all three conclusions were based on partial information and were incomplete.

Is it possible that your child's baseball coach would see something different in him than his piano teacher, or his older sister? So, too, is your view limited.

As parents, we can be like the blind men with their limited understanding, seeing only what's in our immediate field of vision and assuming it's a full picture. After all, is it possible that your child's baseball coach would see something different in him than his piano teacher, or his older sister? So, too, is your view limited.

We can always benefit from a fresh look to help guide us toward what is. My goal is to help you see as full a picture as possible of your child, and, to widen your perspective, you'll need to know the rest of the story.

Although we have not literally lost our sight, like the blind men in the fable, we might as well have blinders on sometimes. It seems to be human nature. How often do we ignore things that we just don't have time to deal with, or try not think about things that make us uncomfortable, hoping that they'll go away if we don't pay them heed?

Everyone will benefit when you shift your perspective, step back, and refocus your lens in order to get as full a picture as possible of who your child is.

Of course, there are challenges with widening your view. In many ways, you can't help but firmly believe you know everything about your child, or that your child behaves, thinks, or reacts in the same ways that you do. Tamsen Firestone, editor-in-chief of the website PsychAlive, stresses that parents can be so tied into their child's identities that any compliment a child receives feels like a compliment to the parent. She explains, "It feels good when someone compliments your child and then adds, 'The apple doesn't fall far from the tree!' Nonetheless, that apple has the seeds for a completely different tree within it. The responsibility of a parent is to nurture those seeds and facilitate the growth of that different tree. The problem is: how can we tell if we are over-identifying with our children? How can we make sure that we are seeing each of them as their own person?"[19]

Everyone will benefit when you shift your perspective, step back, and refocus your lens in order to get as full a picture as possible of who your child is. You may see new things or familiar things in a new light. If you find that you have to swallow your pride at the notion that there might be things you don't see, please do so.

Adopt a Beginner's Mind

The term "beginner's mind" comes from Zen Buddhism, and refers to approaching a subject with openness, curiosity, and a lack of preconceived notions, even when you are not technically a beginner. The beginner's mind can be exactly what we need when widening our perspective. For this purpose, try to forget everything you know about your child. Believing that we already know what we need to know, that we are "experts," prevents us from new discoveries, insights, and surprises. Shunryro Suzuki, the originator of this concept, said, "In the beginner's mind there are many possibilities, but in the expert's there are few."[20] Once we decide we know everything, we shut down opportunities to learn. As parents, we would not intentionally decrease the opportunities to learn about our kids, but that's exactly what we do when we assume we know everything there is to know.

As tempting as it is to focus just on what pleases us, your child has a range of talents, traits, and feelings. "Who he is" includes the things that please you — and the things that don't. To meet our child's need for acceptance, and make acceptance the starting point in our parenting, we must stop looking only at the traits we want to see.

Of course, there are many different reasons why we wear blinders. For example, some parents are uncomfortable with anger. They consider themselves "non-confrontational" and view displaying any anger (or, sometimes, any intense display of emotion) as confrontation. Under this paradigm, anger is to be avoided; otherwise, you give it permission to exist. In actuality, discouraging a child's anger, thereby forcing the child to hide it, does not eliminate the anger; it passes off responsibility to your child to manage this difficult emotion without guidance. He tries to please you by denying his own anger, leaving the feelings unmanaged. Now the parent has missed the opportunity to be effective by helping the child manage his feelings. Instead of developing self-control, the child and everyone in the child's world are controlled by his explosive emotions. In a sense, denying the feelings in your child actually gives those feelings the ultimate power, and forces your child into a lifelong battle to manage them.

One mother became unsettled when her son would erupt in a rage over losing at video games. She dreaded it when he would have friends over, because they would always play video games, and the inevitable meltdown would mortify her. Her way of dealing with her discomfort, however, was to ban video games when friends visited, hoping that if her son were in a calmer environment, his habit of blowing up would disappear.

As parents, we compartmentalize our children, giving center stage to the attributes we like, praising and playing up these "good qualities," and ignoring or denying the negative qualities.

But of course, this unnerved her son even more; she placed blame on the games themselves, turning a blind eye toward the true root of the problem: her son's unmanaged anger. Years later, she realized she might have been so jarred by how fiercely competitive her son was that she tried to avoid anger-provoking situations. She admits that it probably would have been more constructive to explore and understand *why* he was so invested in winning and why his anger, or the intensity of his anger, was so upsetting to her.

Our job as parents is to teach our children to manage *all* of their feelings, not to avoid unpleasant ones. In Part III, we will learn about the importance of stepping up to be the leaders who teach our kids to manage their emotions.

As parents, we compartmentalize our children, giving center stage to the attributes we like, praising and playing up these "good qualities," and ignoring or denying the negative qualities. We succumb to our own PR, believing that what's on center stage is who our child is. But inevitably, the things we ignored and denied will one day come roaring forth, and we are "Shocked, just *shocked*" at our "unrecognizable child."

Bev's son, Christopher, was a golden child in her eyes. He could do no wrong. Temperamentally well matched with each other, they had an easy camaraderie. Christopher was the type of child who never gave his parents a moment's trouble. When he was fifteen, however, Bev received a call from the police that Christopher and three friends had been discovered smoking pot on the roof of an elementary school. The police sent the boys home to their parents with a warning, but Christopher's behavior had shattered the shining image Bev had of him. In her devastation, she cried, "You were the perfect child, and now you've ruined everything!"

Christopher was hardly surprised at his mom's overreaction, and was actually relieved. He had grown up wondering how he could possibly live up to his mother's admiration. Being the golden child had actually felt like an albatross around his neck.

Christopher was fortunate because he welcomed the bursting of his perfection bubble. Many studies and books, such as Robbins' *The Case of the Overachievers: The Secret Lives of Driven Kids*, as mentioned earlier, reveal that other "golden" children grow up and continue to dazzle, but have a dangerous, underlying fear of revealing anything other than perfection. The threat of losing the extravagant praise and approval they're used to keeps them tightly wound.

Lori, another mom, opened up to me about the hell she

and her family went through when her younger daughter Justine turned ten. Up until then, Lori, her husband Bob, and their two daughters, Jessica and Justine, seemed like a perfect little family, both to outsiders and to Lori and Bob. Both girls were good-natured and fairly compliant.

When Justine hit puberty at ten, however, things unraveled quickly. She began to act out, first at school, refusing to follow instructions for simple things like standing in line during gym class. She piled up detentions due to her defiant behavior, and couldn't explain to her parents what was going on. Soon she was cutting and burning herself and threatening suicide.

Bob and Lori felt blindsided — to them, it had all come out of nowhere. They paid attention though, and were able to get Justine effective professional help. They moved her to a school more suited to her needs, and now, eight years later, she is finding her way.

I recently spoke with Lori and was moved by her honesty about the painful road she had traveled to the realization that her daughter's problems did not, in fact, come out of nowhere.

"Justine didn't get much of a chance to be herself growing up, and Bob and I were clueless that we were contributing to that," Lori said. "Jessica had been so easy, and Justine seemed so much like her, so we just took it for granted that things would continue that way. We never really focused on Justine as an individual. It's painful to realize, but we gave her the message that she had better be like Jessica. We basically forced her to hide all her difficult feelings."

Did society hand you your blinders and encourage you to see your child only in terms of her praiseworthy attributes? In *The Curse of the Good Girl*, author Rachel Simmons argues that, while society and parents pressure girls to be "nice, polite, modest and selfless,"[21] no one is nice and sweet all the time. What happens when girls don't act in accordance with this good girl persona? Suddenly they are accused of acting out or misbehaving. Perhaps, like Justine, they are acting out what we have refused to acknowledge all along (with our blinders on), or anything that doesn't fit into the good girl persona that we construct for them.

It may seem counterintuitive, but "perfect" children should actually be encouraged to express and become familiar with their negativity, fear, and other, less than desirable feelings, in order to prevent them from losing touch with these very real parts of who they are.

For instance, if you have a young child who may show some "golden" characteristics, encourage her to speak openly with you about her anxiety, fears, or negative feelings as well as her successes and joys. Tell her she can come to you to talk out her feelings of jealousy toward a classmate, or her frustrations with her siblings. With this openness between you, you can better coach her in processing and developing mastery over her actions. Show her that you don't expect her to be perfect and that she doesn't have to constantly please others.

Be Emotionally Present

If you want to really know your child and have him open up to you, you must be emotionally present. By doing so, you give your child permission to show all of himself to you. What does it mean to be emotionally present? It means letting our children communicate all their feelings, not just the pleasant ones. It can be a challenge to be present with children who feel sad, angry, or incompetent, but it is worth the effort (and is the only way you can teach them appropriate ways to express difficult emotions). If your child senses that you want to know her thoughts, feelings, and beliefs, she will let you know in words. Let your child reveal the full picture of who she is by making it clear that you want to know everything about her and can handle whatever she has to tell you, not just the good stuff.

When parents give the impression that they do not want to know the bad stuff, their children will often express their struggles by acting out, rather than talking. Notice what your child is telling you through his behavior. For instance, if he is terrified of giving a report in front of his class, he may not necessarily tell you; what you may see instead is your child bullying his younger sibling. We should be tuning into not just what is said, but what is *unsaid*, perhaps as you see him having moments of quiet sadness by himself before going to school.

Mark Goulston, MD, a psychiatrist who focuses on the importance of listening, has compiled a list of the things he has heard teenagers say to their parents. Goulston shared the experience of one father, a CEO, who had believed that his teenage son was lazy and blowing it in high school. Dr. Goulston surprised him by telling him that *he* was the one who was blowing it by not tuning into his son's pain, and suggested he give his son the list and ask what applied to him:

> "Well I gave it to him, he read it and I asked him what applied to him. He looked at me...no, actually he looked right through me and narrowed his eyes in a hostile manner and said, 'All of it.' I then said to him, 'Why didn't you tell me it was so bad?' And he replied firmly, but less hostile [sic], 'Because *you* didn't *f*%king want to know!*'" [22]

When parents ignore what's going on beneath the surface, it can lead to negative consequences later on. Julianne Idleman writes poignantly about how her father begged her to stop her loud crying when she was four years old, something that left a lasting imprint:

> Forty years later, what has stayed with me is the deeply jarring alienation brought on by my father's inability to cope with, let alone understand, my emotional experience. He just wanted it to stop. How could my father, who I adored beyond words, plead with me not to express an experience that clearly needed his comforting and attention? Shame and confusion were layered over whatever the original hurt may have been. If my father complained that I no longer told him anything when I was a teen, he was reaping seeds he planted when I was very small and needed him to listen.[23]

If connecting emotionally with your child is a challenge for you, it's crucial for your child's well-being that you find a way to do so. Chapter 7 will delve deeper into ways to make this emotional connection work for people who may be less in tune with their feelings.

Being present and listening when children are experiencing strong emotions is pivotal in creating a strong parent-child connection. Yes, this might mean listening openheartedly to your child's wails of rage, instead of banishing him to time out to cool off alone. Early on in your child's life, a strong parent-child connection during moments of heightened emotional intensity has been called the "super-protective factor" against negative outcomes in adolescence[24] — the time when your child may experience a torrent of new emotions. Having a close connected relationship with a caring adult, one who listens to the child's feelings, is the single strongest indicator that an adolescent will reach adulthood without experiencing teen pregnancy or violence, without becoming addicted to drugs or tobacco, and without dropping out of high school. Emotional presence is the key to that connection. Don't tell your child his feelings are right or wrong. Don't tell him what to feel or what not to feel. Acknowledge his feelings but don't try to fix things.

Being present and listening when children are experiencing strong emotions is pivotal in creating a strong parent-child connection.

This is something Helena, mom to seventeen-year-old Aidan, can relate to. She shared her "aha!" moment that Aidan was not only transforming into his own person, but also that her support was crucial to him coming to terms with his new emotions in a healthy way. The moment came when Aidan was in middle school.

"The first time you realize you can't dictate everything they do is shocking. There was this one day when we had a big, *huge* fight. I don't even remember what it was about, and you never can. But what I remember is that he wasn't going to back down and neither was I. He was his own little person and he was going to believe the reasons why he was right, as was I." That moment, when she saw him as a growing person who simply needed validation for his feelings and perspective proved to be pivotal in strengthening their relationship.

This type of emotional presence can also affect your child

at a very early age. Children know intuitively when they don't have your undivided attention, and even toddlers and babies know when you are emotionally in sync. Maggie Day Conran, of the blog "No Mommy Brain," wrote about her infant son, Finn, who awoke screaming and crying in the night:

> On this particular night his screams were so shrill and desperate that I had to go to him. He sounded terrified or hurt or like something was definitely wrong. Why else would someone go from sound asleep to screaming without so much as a pause in between? I opened the door to his warm room cooing, "Baby, baby, baby, what is it?" He caught his breath and stood up and reached for me in the dark. I lifted him out of his crib and held his tiny body close to mine as he wailed and squirmed and patted my back. "Finny, honey, you're okay. You're *okay*. Mama's here. Mama's here..." But his screams didn't stop and he was practically throwing himself out of my arms. Finally, in the still of the night, I heard him. Loud and clear. He *wasn't* okay. I may not have known what was wrong but no one screams like that if they're okay. How frustrating it must be to feel one thing and have someone you love and trust keep telling you the opposite. So I switched sides.
>
> "Finny's sad," I said in my most matter-of-fact voice. "Finn hurts." As I spoke to him, he instantly quieted down. He rested his head softly on my shoulder as I continued to put words to what he might be feeling. "Finn's so upset. Finny's scared..." It felt like as soon as I stopped fighting him ("You're okay" vs. "NO I'M NOT!"), he was able to come to terms with what he was feeling and let it go.[25]

Even though Maggie's intention from the start was to comfort and support her child, she couldn't help him until she realized the bottom line: that Finn *needed* to express his upset emotions, and she could not simply shush them away.

Give Time, Undivided Attention

The number one way to gain an authentic picture of your child's emotions, passions, disposition, and outlook on life is to let your child be the one to show you who he or she is! Although it may sound simplistic, it actually requires a commitment: if you want your child to show you who he is, you need to give him time and undivided attention. Engage with him; don't parent from the sidelines. O.A. Battista, a Canadian-American author, said something quite lovely: "The best inheritance a parent can give to his children is a few minutes of his time each day." Let your son or daughter know you're in his corner, that you have his back, that you are his honest, respectful counsel and pillar of support. How do you do this?

Let's start by looking at how *not* to bond with your child.

While standing in line at a Starbucks, a twenty-something-year-old mother with an infant in a stroller stood behind me. Mom was on the phone talking, as her baby cooed adorably and smiled at anyone who would give her eye contact. Meanwhile, mom was not at all engaged with her baby. Although she ended the call before she placed her order, she soon made another, and was chatting away as she left.

As I watched, I pondered the cumulative effect of every small moment when parents are physically present with their baby, but mentally engaged elsewhere. They are there, but not there for their child.

The time you spend intentionally engaged with your child should be free of distractions. You're not engaging with your child if you're texting. You're not engaging with your child if you're reading email or taking calls — you're distracted, and kids *know* when they're second priority. Don't ever think you're fooling them. The flip side of this is the powerful statement you make to your child when you make them a priority. Declaring, "Honey, I'm turning off my cell phone so we're not interrupted," or saying to a friend, "Sorry, I can't meet you for coffee — I always have special time with my daughter on early release Wednesdays," lets your child know your interaction with her is a valued part of your life.

When you spend connected time with your child, you have the opportunity to uncover more about what makes him tick.

Another way to make the most out of your one-on-one time is to ground it in something that your child loves, or is super-interested in. This is important for many reasons. For one, when we're with our kids, it's easy to fall into the pattern of taking care of business: the quarterly report card, or responsibilities at home, for instance. Take the initiative and offer, "I'll leave the dishes till later so you can show me what you learned at soccer camp before it gets dark outside." This not only gives you the opportunity to experience firsthand what your child is passionate about, but it also shows him that you value his interests. It shows your child that you *want* to know different sides of him, and that each of those aspects is what makes your child special.

When you spend connected time with your child, you have the opportunity to uncover more about what makes him tick. This is how I learned something about my son Ethan that was invaluable in helping him become the best version of who he is. He was very bright, and scored high on the standardized tests, so, naturally, I expected he would be a top-performing student. But he didn't care about excelling, and I wasn't thrilled about that. My husband Carl was much more relaxed about grades, so I took his lead and didn't make a big deal about "living up to his potential," which helped keep our relationship warm and connected.

Yet, it was confusing to me, and Ethan sensed that. One day, he explained it. He didn't put in much effort academically, he said, because he focused on one thing at a time. Baseball took up his energy and focus. He cared about being the best at baseball, and that's where his intense effort went. "Someday, when I'm not playing baseball, I'll put in the time and effort academically," he told me. It was not how I would have approached life, but hearing it from him made perfect sense as *his* way of being. And it's exactly how he is leading his life.

I recommend directly asking your child questions about who they are. You probably won't have success here if it comes out of the blue, but why not play a game with your child where you take turns filling in the blanks in sentences, such as:

- Something very few people know about me is_____.

- I wish someone noticed _____ about me.

- When I _____, I feel most like ME.

- I wish people would not criticize me for _____.

- _____ makes me so happy!

Once you warm your child up to the idea that you are his source of undivided time and attention, you can move onto the next step: creating a relationship based on emotional support.

One thing I must caution about, as I mentioned earlier in this book, is that it's easy to get overwhelmed by the profusion of parenting books (irony noted) and parenting information and advice on the Internet.

Jacky Howell, an early-childhood education expert in the Washington, D.C. area, identifies with this.

"How would I know necessarily what's a more valid resource? If I'm a parent, how would I know that? I've often said to parents, I can go to a bookstore and look at a shelf about discipline and pick up a book and it will say do this and pick up the book next to it and it says don't do this. There's nothing wrong with that. For some children you do this, and for others you don't do this. It really is individualized. It's helping families see those individual differences. Families were kind of taught a little bit in our society that one size fits all, and it's not necessarily true. What works for one child doesn't always work for another child."

It's so crucial to start with your child and from your child.

"Enlisten" Help

Sometimes, for whatever reason, or through circumstances beyond our control, it is difficult for us to understand our child. Engaging can be hard. A beginner's mind and an engaged presence can make a big difference, but if you feel you still need to open your view a bit wider, try "enlistening," or *enlisting* others to help you *listen* to perspectives that may provide valuable insight about your child.

In some families, neither parent understands a child. Carlos was raised in a large family in Queens, New York. He describes himself as someone his relatives view with confusion.

"I feel like I'm the most loved but also the most misunderstood. I think it's mainly the way I think and the stuff I'm into," reflected Carlos, who, much to his mother's chagrin, is an actor. He continued, "The way I have my head in the clouds upsets them. Even as a kid I would daydream all the time. I'd get lost in my imagination and they'd kind of want me to come back down. Their personalities are different from mine but not necessarily bad. They're very outspoken, with very strong personalities."

These differences assert themselves particularly at big family gatherings. "They always get me to talk more. For example, if I'm quiet they assume I'm upset or sad, and they try to cheer me up. I'm comfortable in my silence, and they're not comfortable in silence at all. 'No one is supposed to be like this,' they say. I think they won't admit it, but they're all trying to make me more like them." He laughed. "I think I'm trying to find a way to say it without sounding like I'm complaining! But that's the truth — they don't get me."

Carlos explained that his mother still has a hard time grappling with his life choices, even though she would pay for every acting class, every headshot, every book of monologues. "She lets me know every step of the way that, for a long time, she was waiting for me to wake up. But, I feel like I would have known I was meant to be an actor much sooner had they encouraged my way of thinking a little more."

Despite feeling misunderstood by his parents, one person in Carlos' life was the key to his feeling accepted: his late uncle.

"My uncle is a lot of the reason why my mom is scared of my life choices," Carlos explained. "He was very smart, very artsy. He always wanted to be behind the camera, or be a journalist. He had an awesome soul to him, but he got into drugs and fell in love young and that threw off his trajectory, I think. But, he got me because, minus the trajectory his life took, he pretty much *is* me. He thought the way I thought and we would talk about movies and comic books. It's funny: my mom was saying the other day that he would always talk to her about me, saying, 'V, please, let him live his life!' Even though my mom financially did way more for me than he ever could or did, I think in those conversations, he didn't just support my idea of being an actor; he understood it."

The childhood of my friend Liz echoes Carlos' experience. Both grew up feeling as if they didn't belong in their families. Liz told me, "It wasn't okay to be me. I didn't seem to fit my parents' expectations for a girl. I excelled at math and science, and loved to build things and figure out how things worked. My sister, on the other hand, won the hearts of my parents by being quite girly." Her parents didn't encourage her interest in technical subjects, even though her dad was an engineer. He told Liz he would never hire a female engineer in his firm, because "they were too emotional." Unable to reconcile who she was with who her parents wanted her to be, she struggled to find a career path. "I began in medicine (studying to become a psychiatrist), then got an art degree, then studied massage therapy, before finally settling on physics." Along the way, she struggled with depression and lost the will to live, which prompted counseling and helped her to begin to understand her family.

"I moved to the West Coast and started a professional life

as a laser engineer and, later, a thermal analyst. It was a healthy choice to achieve some distance (both physical and psychological) from my parents, and I learned to build a fairly satisfying life without them. But it still bothered me that I could be so different and so unaccepted. How could I be genetically related to them? I still wanted to understand and longed for a familial connection."

Then, four years ago, her father's mother passed away, and, at the funeral, Liz met her Uncle Jerry. He had been long estranged from the family, and was rarely spoken of. Imagine Liz's surprise to learn that she and Uncle Jerry were cut from the same cloth! Like Liz, Uncle Jerry had worked as a thermal analyst in the aerospace field. Like Liz, Uncle Jerry loved muscle cars. "The more we talked, the more we discovered we had in common," she told me excitedly. "For the first time, I could see myself in another family member. It was a revelation."

Finding each other was significant for Jerry as well, because the next summer he invited Liz to a vintage car club event at a race track. "Not only did he want my company, but he also wanted me to drive the track. All that weekend, he gently mentored me, teaching me how to improve my driving skills and asking me to help with small car tune-up tasks. He believed in my abilities, and the fact that I was a woman wasn't a deficit; it was cool."

As I listened to Liz recount this wonderful story about connecting with her uncle, I knew that I would include it in my book. She finished on a wistful note. "I'm grateful for this affirming experience with Jerry as an adult. But it also makes me wonder how my life would have been different if he had stayed near the family and been a part of my life growing up. I think he would have encouraged my interest in science and engineering and given me some of the positive attention I so much wanted from my own parents."

Would it make sense for you to "enlisten" others for support or a second perspective? Everyone sees your child from a different perspective, and other people who know your child may have useful information. Asking uncles, aunts, neighbors, teachers, coaches, godparents, other siblings, the mother of your daughter's best friend, or *anyone* who has a good relationship with your child to provide their point of view is a great way to "enlisten" help. Ask them what your child is like when they are around them, or to think of something your child has done or said that is very telling about who your child is. Ask them what your child has said to them about *you!* You may come across some enlightening bits of information. And the beauty of it is that all you have to do is ask.

The teenaged son of a friend of mine would hang out at his friend's house constantly. After several years, the moms became close and started sharing information and anecdotes about their boys. My friend was stunned to find out that her son had been teaching his friend study skills and strategies to help him manage some learning disabilities. She had never seen this helpful side of her son. It helped her enormously in understanding who her son was.

Teachers are in an especially strong position to be the one person who understands a child, and the best ones intuitively understand this power. A teacher not only speaks to your child in a refreshingly different way from how you do, but also observes how your child interacts with her peers. A friend of mine offered this recollection to me when we discussed the power of teachers to make a difference in the lives of their students.

She had witnessed a teenager with morally strict parents

choose excessively high-risk behavior. He had a serious problem with drug and alcohol abuse, was sexually promiscuous, and had behaved brazenly and outspokenly in class. My friend (his teacher) suspected it was a possible rebellion against his parents, both of whom are teachers.

Ultimately, it was a rebellion that he paid for — the young man became incarcerated, dropped out of high school, and went to rehab. She asked permission from the parents to write to him, suspecting it would help him if she sent him *The Question Holds the Lantern,* by John Donohue, an inspirational essay she teaches in her humanities class. Years later, the young man visited her, relaying how this piece of literature helped him find some answers. Looking back at this student's darkest moments, she realized she would have been thrilled to share her perspective with his parents, had they asked.

The "listen" part of "enlistening" is just as important as the "enlist" part. When you get feedback, listen to it and reflect on it! It's all too easy to discount the things we don't want to hear. However, remember why you're asking: to get a fuller, more realistic picture of your child. Also, keep in mind that some of the feedback you receive may not necessarily be comforting or positive. While it may be unsettling, it's important to remember that revelations are what you're looking for, and will help guide you to a more complete, fresh view of who your child is.

When you get feedback, listen to it and reflect on it! It's all too easy to discount the things we don't want to hear.

What about when you receive negative feedback about your child without asking for it? Pay attention anyway. While many parents are quick to switch into Mama Bear mode and defend their child — especially in cases where the knee-jerk reaction is that the person speaking had no business giving an opinion in the first place — try to keep an eye open for repeated complaints. Step out of your story, if need be, to take in the information.

Terry had a mean streak, but she was also wily and good at hiding it. She would hurt her siblings. Yet, her mother Joyce had a story that prevented her from taking in any information about her daughter that was negative. In Joyce's mind, Terry could do no wrong, so she would dismiss the complaints from neighbors as silly and the concerns from her playmates' mothers as jealousy. Her over-identification with her daughter kept her in denial, even in the face of repeated red flags.

If you're seeing a pattern in the comments, pay attention.

Joyce's inability to step in when her daughter desperately needed a parent's guidance ended up affecting everyone in the family and created a ripple effect that was far-reaching.

If you're seeing a pattern in the comments, pay attention. If your son is rarely invited back to his friends' homes, or has trouble holding onto friendships, pay attention. Ask yourself if there are things you may have failed to notice.

Now that you've looked at your child with a beginner's mind and, perhaps, stepped out of your story, it's time to gather your insights and learn how to recognize which aspects of your child are parts of the CoreSelf.

Exercise

Fill out the following worksheet with as many descriptive words as you can about your child. Try not to judge what you write. Just keep writing. In the next chapter, your descriptions will help you ascertain your child's CoreSelf.

_____

_____

_____

_____

_____

_____

_____

_____

_____

_____

_____

_____

_____

_____

_____

_____

_____

_____

Chapter 5: Accepting Who Your Child Is: the CoreSelf

"One of the most generous gifts you can give your child is to study her temperament, and once you've learned it, work to accept it." — Wendy Mogel

Now that you have a fuller picture of your child, let's look at which aspects have been apparent from the earliest days. Children come to us with their own way of being in, and interacting with, the world, and each individual has a unique potpourri of innate characteristics. It's important to remember that some aspects of your child's temperament show up *from day one*. This is the place to start when looking at who your child is.

What Is the CoreSelf?

In leading with acceptance, I use the term CoreSelf to describe those aspects of a person that are present at birth and unlikely to change over the course of the person's lifetime. Leading with acceptance incorporates the latest findings in biology, psychology, and brain science, but the concept of CoreSelf is a TOOL for understanding, not a statement of fact. There are many valid theories of what constitutes core essence, nature, personality, or temperament. A pivotal work, the New York Longitudinal Study by psychiatrists Alexander Thomas and Stella Chess, found nine temperament traits that were identifiable at birth or soon after, and remained relatively stable throughout life.[26] I use their nine traits as the starting point for the concept of CoreSelf,[27] but other valuable models include the Myers-Briggs Temperament Indicator[28] and Michael Gurian's Core Personality, as described in his book *Nurture the Nature.*[29]

The Nine Traits of the CoreSelf

An individual's unique grouping of nine inborn temperament traits that are present in all people makes up the first part of the CoreSelf. These are the nine innate traits[30] of the CoreSelf:

1. Activity
2. Adaptability
3. Distractibility
4. Ease with the Unfamiliar
5. Intensity
6. Optimism
7. Persistence
8. Regularity
9. Sensory Reactivity

Let's take a look at each of the nine inborn temperament traits and how they show up in children:

ACTIVITY refers to the amount of physical movement a person engages in over time.
Parents cannot change a child's innate preference for activity.
- LOW ACTIVITY: Andrés spends a lot of time cuddled into

a big chair with his books and loves taking long car trips. He falls asleep and wakes up the next morning in the same position.

- HIGH ACTIVITY: Simi's parents can't take her to the mall because she detests sitting in the stroller, and, when she walks, she bolts toward whatever catches her eye. She pops up to dance when she hears music, and, during story time at the library, she gets too restless to sit still.

ADAPTABILITY refers to the flexibility and resistance a person has to changes in routines, plans, and their environment.
Parents cannot change a child's innate level of adaptability.

- LOW ADAPTABILITY: Matthew enjoys going to the same park every Saturday, and gets angry when his parents want to try a new one. He loves his own crib and has great difficulty sleeping anywhere else.
- HIGH ADAPTABILITY: Raj is four years old and has already traveled around the world with his parents. He sleeps on planes, trains, and automobiles — wherever he happens to be when he gets tired.

DISTRACTIBILITY is how well a person can tune out interruptions and outside stimuli.
Parents cannot change a child's innate level of distractibility.

- LOW DISTRACTIBILITY: At the park, Kyla heads right to the sandbox and is content to play there, even when all the other kids go to the swings or monkey bars.
- HIGH DISTRACTIBILITY: Cameron, Kyla's fraternal twin, also loves the sandbox, but, after a few minutes of sand play, he runs off to join the other children climbing, sliding, and exploring.

EASE WITH THE UNFAMILIAR refers to how bold or hesitant a person's initial reaction is to new, unfamiliar people, places, foods, and other stimuli.

Parents cannot change a child's innate ease with the unfamiliar.

- LOW EASE WITH THE UNFAMILIAR: When a new babysitter comes to the house, Rosie hides. She is shy. Once she is introduced, however, her parents have noticed that she warms up quickly.

- HIGH EASE WITH THE UNFAMILIAR: Rosie's younger brother, Derrick, is the opposite. He immediately invites every new visitor to take a tour of the backyard and check out the chicken coop he helped his mom build.

INTENSITY is the energy level of a person's responses, irrespective of whether the response is positive or negative.

Parents cannot change a child's innate intensity level.

- LOW INTENSITY: Sebastian's nickname is "Mr. Mellow." Even during his "terrible twos," nothing seemed to ruffle his feathers much.

- HIGH INTENSITY: Moira has strong feelings about just about everything. She will sob on her bed when her feelings are hurt, and she will jump for joy when she's happy. No one ever has to guess how she's feeling.

OPTIMISM refers to general pattern of outlook on life.

Parents cannot change a child's innate disposition.

- LOW OPTIMISM: Gemma has a serious demeanor and prefers to think through everything that might go wrong when she plans her actions.

- HIGH OPTIMISM: Natalie smiles easily and frequently, and wonders why her sister Gemma is "so negative." She wakes up every morning in a good mood, ready to take on the day.

PERSISTENCE refers to a person's stick-to-it-iveness when faced with challenges.

Parents cannot change a child's innate persistence.

- LOW PERSISTENCE: Mars tries to jam the pieces of his wooden puzzles and, when they don't fit, he throws them across the room and picks up another toy to play with.
- HIGH PERSISTENCE: Seth is determined to stack all his blocks in a tower, starting over every time they tumble, until he figures out how to balance the last few.

REGULARITY refers to the predictability of a person's eating, sleeping, and eliminating.

Parents cannot change a child's innate level of regularity.

- LOW REGULARITY: Eliana has never been on any kind of schedule, despite her parents' attempts. She is frequently not hungry at mealtimes or sleepy at bedtime.
- HIGH REGULARITY: Anjali seems to have an internal clock that wakes her at the same time every morning. She eats three meals and two snacks and is in bed at 7:30 every night.

SENSORY REACTIVITY refers to the level at which a person ignores or is bothered by external stimuli such as sounds, light, temperature, textures, and tastes.

Parents cannot change a child's innate level of sensitivity.

- LOW SENSORY REACTIVITY: Tiana has always been able to sleep through commotion. She doesn't pay much attention to the clothes her mom dresses her in and rarely fusses when she has a wet diaper.
- HIGH SENSORY REACTIVITY: Garrett gets headaches from scented soaps and shampoos and won't eat any foods

with a mushy texture. He says jeans are uncomfortable and will only wear sweatpants and cotton turtlenecks.

Every trait, whether low or high, carries opportunities and challenges. But because parents are human, we do indeed react to others' traits through the filter of our own temperament and life experience, which leads to judgments.

Your first reaction to some of the descriptions may be that they are good or bad, but there is no right or wrong score on the trait gradients. Every trait, whether low or high, carries opportunities and challenges. But because parents are human, we do indeed react to others' traits through the filter of our own temperament and life experience, which leads to judgments. In order to raise the Child You've Got, you must become aware of and try to let go of your judgments. Looking at the opportunities and challenges inherent in the CoreSelf traits will help, as you lead with acceptance, guiding the Child You've Got child toward becoming the best version of who she is.

Challenges and Opportunities in the CoreSelf Traits

Kim John Payne, the author of *Simplicity Parenting*, has described how our children's natural quirkiness becomes a gift, if balanced, or a disorder, if stressed.[31] If you want to make sure your child's traits develop in a balanced fashion, accept them, and lead your child, as described in Part III.

Level of Trait	Challenges	Opportunities
Low Activity	Hard to rush, not prone to exercise, can seem "pokey"	Sits quietly for long periods, relaxed, self-contained
High Activity	Difficulty sitting still/relaxing	Productive
Low Adaptability	Unwilling to try new things	Happy with the status quo
High Adaptability	Susceptible to impulsivity	Low maintenance, socially adept
Low Distractibility	Can seem tuned out	Focused, can study in noisy surroundings
High Distractibility	Poor follow through, needs quiet to study	Good multi-tasker
Low Ease with the Unfamiliar	Requires patient introductions	Discerning
High Ease with the Unfamiliar	Lacks discernment	Open to new possibilities
Low Intensity	Can seem unmoved, uncaring, easy to ignore	Maintains cool under pressure
High Intensity	Can seem like crying wolf, draining to be around	Emotionally expressive, unlikely to be ignored
Low Optimism	Pessimism can wear on people	Voice of reason, measured approach
High Optimism	Cheeriness may seem insincere	Easy to have around, well-liked
Low Persistence	Gives up easily	Tries lots of things
High Persistence	Annoying	Stick-to-it-ativeness
Low Regularity	Unpredictable	Spontaneous
High Regularity	Rigid	Predictable
Low Sensory Reactivity	Oblivious	Not finicky
High Sensory Reactivity	Finicky	Observant

The Light of the CoreSelf

The second part of the CoreSelf is not as definable as the first, with its nine traits. It is your child's *light*. Whereas the nine traits indicate how your child reacts to and lives in the world, your child's light represents the unique gifts he brings to the world. It is akin to thinking of your child in terms of what kind of *soul* he is. Your child's light might be explained as the reason why "the whole is greater than the sum of its parts."

"I am meant to shine, as children do. I was born to make manifest
the glory of God that is within me." — Marianne Williamson

We are meant to shine. Our light reveals itself as the singular, special spark within each of us. Embodied at birth, it is as unique as our DNA blueprint. Whether it is called essence, God's breath or glory, eternal soul, or original flame, we are all, without exception, born with this light. Each new life is full of promise and potential, showing up in a baby's first breath and first smile, and the sweet, gradual unveiling of a child's tender soul.

Your child's light represents the unique gifts he brings to the world. It is akin to thinking of your child in terms of what kind of *soul* he is.

This light remains with us as long as we are alive. Although it may not blaze all the time, it is there, as long as there is breath. When the breath finally leaves the body, it's as if the light goes along. So, if we're each born with our own light, and the light is there all during our lives, then why do some people absolutely shine and others show hardly a flicker? Why do some of us seem to be lit from within and others barely glow? I believe it is the ability to live in alignment with our CoreSelf that allows our light to radiate, from deep within, out into the world. When our CoreSelf is understood and accepted (and, ideally, admired) by those who care for us, we are given license to shine.

Make no mistake, *every* child has his own light, no matter how difficult or defiant or unlikeable he or she might seem. Because children form their own identity based on what we mirror to them, it is incumbent on parents to identify the spark and reflect it back.

Make no mistake, *every* child has his own light, no matter how difficult or defiant or unlikeable he or she might seem.

Your child's light might be reflected in her mathematical genius, or her athletic grace. It could be in any talent or aptitude that is obvious, or one that is more subtle. Your child's light could be his shy smile that melts the hearts of everyone who sees it, or it might show in your daughter's hilarious mimicry of the adults in her life. Some children have a deep sensitivity to the underdog or an uncanny ability to see both sides of every disagreement. These bright spots of light may or may not show up on the traits assessment, but they are just as important in defining who your child is. Recognizing and nurturing this light will help your child understand and develop the unique gifts he has to share.

You've heard plenty about the intensity of my son, Jordan. His younger brother, Ethan, in contrast, is a calm soul. As Ethan grew up, he showed great interest in cooking, and began to watch TV cooking shows. Although I have *zero* interest in cooking, I would sit with him while he watched. We bonded.

He saw me making his interests a priority, and I witnessed Ethan's love of cooking, and creating, who his favorite chefs were and why, and so much more about what makes him tick. I would often sit with him for half an hour in the afternoon. He would open up. I would ask him questions like, "Does that interest you?" and he would say, "No, I don't like baking as much because you have to be too precise."

"Why do you like that chef?"

"He beats everyone at *Iron Chef*."

With this, I begin to see how his competitiveness combines with his creativity and why he would be into *Iron Chef*. As I entered his world, I began to recognize his own unique light expressed in cooking. Now that he has graduated from college, he has decided to make a career out of this passion.

What Does "Accept the CoreSelf" Mean?

Maybe you've followed everything up until now, but you find yourself wondering, "What exactly does 'accept' mean?" Accept means that you understand that something cannot be changed. It does not mean you like it, or condone it. It simply means you can embrace it as something that "is."

You will find that, the more you commit to seeing your child with a fresh pair of eyes, the easier it will be to get to know him. You'll gain a deeper understanding of who your child is at his core, and what he needs in order to truly shine. The CoreSelf is the essence of your child as he was born, and is what you must embrace as what is.

In the next chapter, you'll gain some understanding of how to know, when looking at the "hotspots" you experience with your child, what relates to CoreSelf, and what relates to behavior. And, you'll learn how to manage each.

Exercise

On the following chart, use an X to indicate your assessment of your child's level of each trait. It may help to refer back to the descriptions you wrote of your child from Chapter 4.

EXAMPLE: My child's CoreSelf Activity is:

	Lowest Level	Mid-Level	Highest Level
Activity			X

	Lowest Level	Mid-Level	Highest Level
Activity			
Adaptability			
Distractibility			
Ease with Unfamiliar			
Intensity			
Optimism			
Persistence			
Regularity			
Sensory Reactivity			

Chapter 6: Separating the CoreSelf from Behavior

"God, grant me the serenity to accept the things I cannot change, courage to change the things I can, and wisdom to know the difference." — Reinhold Niebur

We accept the CoreSelf so we don't make children wrong for being who they are. But how do we accomplish this in the real-life trenches of parenting? Conflicts arise; parents and children react and over-react. Conflict escalates. Amid all the friction and stirred up emotions, how can you know what is related to the CoreSelf and what is not? What are you able to accept when you are so angry you think you might explode?

Let's be clear about something essential: accepting your child's CoreSelf does not mean you should accept bad behavior. In fact, the opposite is true — you should never accept bad behavior, and it is your responsibility as a parent to teach your child how to behave properly. The distinction between the CoreSelf and behavior is therefore crucial. In leading with acceptance, we work hard to differentiate between the two, because, while you cannot control who your child is, you do have enormous influence over how your child expresses who he is.

Let's be clear about something essential: accepting your child's CoreSelf does not mean you should accept bad behavior.

Behavior

Behavior is learned responses, or the actions by which a living organism adapts to its environment — as opposed to *instincts* and *reflexes*. It refers to the way we interact with our environment, not how we feel or process information or think.

How we behave is the product of who we are, as affected by our experiences in the world. This behavior is learned, and can be unlearned. Our job as parents is to shape our children's behavior, but within the context of complete acceptance of who they are at their core. The lovely paradox is that, by accepting "what is," we are in the best position to channel "what is" in a positive direction. With acceptance, you will be able view your child's traits more objectively, which will allow you to guide him toward the best version of himself.

Equally important, when you accept who your child is, you create a strong parent-child connection that empowers you to be a real leader in your family. Children who love and respect their parents naturally want to emulate them. Leaders who are respected can effectively teach not only proper behavior, but also values and morals. Isn't this what we want as parents?

Hotspots

In leading with acceptance, the recurring problems between parents and children are hotspots, and, collectively, they are seen as a barometer of the parent-child relationship. Some of the most common hotspots include:

- Meltdowns/temper tantrums
- Sibling rivalry/hitting/fighting
- Defiance/disrespect/angry interactions/talking back
- Fighting/bullying/aggression
- Not listening to parents/refusing to do chores, turn off computers, or go to bed
- School and homework issues
- Honesty/lying/manipulation

As we discussed in Part I, when problems recur and parents find themselves on the hamster wheel, there is often an underlying issue that is not being addressed. When children do not feel accepted, it will eventually manifest in their behavior, and if parents do not address the underlying issue, these hotspots will burn them both. To lead with acceptance, we analyze hotspots to make sure we understand what role the CoreSelf is playing, and what role learned behavior is playing. After all, this is where it's all too easy to make a child feel wrong for being who he is.

When children do not feel accepted, it will eventually manifest in their behavior, and if parents do not address the underlying issue, these hotspots will burn them both.

Our goal is to separate out the child's behavior from the child's CoreSelf.

Review the worksheet you prepared in Chapter 5, where you measured your child's nine traits of the CoreSelf. We'll be referring to it as we learn the difference between the CoreSelf and behavior.

The following four questions are designed to help you deal with hotpots by separating out what must be accepted from what must be guided:

1. *What is the hotspot?* Describe the recurring conflict.
2. *What does that look like?* Beyond value judgments, describe who, what, where, when, and why.
3. *What role do CoreSelf traits play in the hotspot?* Acknowledge and accept this part.
4. *What role does learned behavior play in the hotspot?* Take responsibility to be a leader and guide this part.

Since raising Jordan was the catalyst for my leading with acceptance, let's use him as an example. You already know that he was seven months old when I had the epiphany about the importance of accepting him for who he was. I had a deep knowing that accepting who he was had to be the first step in my parenting, or else he would feel wrong for being who he was. It was a blessed, life-changing realization. But as Jordan became a toddler, and then a preschooler, it became glaringly obvious that the intensity of his moods was controlling our family. "As Jordan goes, so goes the family" was an accurate description of our household, and I was concerned that this did not portend well for how he would grow up. I didn't want him to learn to control people by crying and carrying on, or to believe that he was in charge and that the world revolved around him. And yet, in some ways, this was becoming his experience.

Jordan's frequent tantrums were difficult to stop. He would become upset about something, and he could not or would not let it go. Telling him no at the grocery store when he spied some junk food he wanted, or at Target when he desperately wanted a new Ninja Turtle for his collection, invariably led to long and protracted periods of crying, screaming, and thrashing. At times, it wasn't clear why he was upset, but the intense expression of his feelings and his endless persistence were the common denominator in all these episodes.

One day, as I was standing in the lobby of his preschool to pick him up, he walked out, saw me waiting, and plopped down on the floor smack dab in the middle of this busy traffic area. He refused to get up and would not talk about what was on his mind, so, after my futile attempts, I told him I would be picking him up and carrying him to the car. Amid the wide-eyed stares of the other moms and preschoolers, I did my best to get us out of the lobby as he thrashed and bucked in my arms. He would not accept hugs, gentle touch, or comforting words. He raged as I buckled him into the car seat, and continued during the twenty-minute ride, falling asleep just as we pulled into the driveway at home.

Here's how the four questions helped me analyze this hotspot:

1.   *What was the hotspot?* The hotspot was his intense meltdowns. He threw a fit whenever he was told no.

2.   *What did that look like?* It happened when his dad or I told him no. It did not occur with the babysitter, his

grandparents, or teacher. It was not a gradual build-up of frustration; the moment he got frustrated, he would explode with loud screams and crying. Once this happened, he could not be soothed, comforted, or reasoned with. It happened frequently at home, as well as in public.

3.   *What role do Jordan's CoreSelf traits play in the hotspot?*

	Lowest Level	Mid-Level	Highest Level

Activity N/A

Adaptability   X
> Low adaptability meant he did not adjust easily to changes.

Distractibility   X
> Low distractibility meant his attention couldn't be shifted easily.

Ease with Unfamiliar N/A

Intensity   X
> High intensity meant he expressed himself dramatically.

Optimism   X
> Low optimism meant he did not look on the bright side.

Persistence   X
> High persistence meant he would not give up.

Regularity N/A

Sensory Reactivity N/A

Reminder! You cannot discipline, punish, or teach these traits out of your child. When you accept that your child has these traits, you will be in a position to help your child manage these traits to be effective in the world.

4. What role does learned behavior play in the hotspot?

His actions are his way of expressing his intense feelings. He has learned to express these feelings (anger, frustration, discomfort) in this way. It certainly gets our attention and sometimes, wanting desperately for him to stop, we give in.

Leading with Acceptance:

Answering these questions allowed me to see the major role that Jordan's CoreSelf played in these interactions. His low adaptability, low distractibility, high intensity, low optimism, and high persistence were part of who he was, and were not going to change. But how he acted in response to being triggered could and needed to change. Once I understood what I needed to accept and what I needed to guide, I talked to him:

> "Jordan, one of the special things about you is how deeply you feel your feelings *(accept CoreSelf trait)*. I love that you feel your feelings BIG, BIG, BIG! When you're happy, you laugh so hard it makes me smile, too. When you have angry feelings, you feel them BIG, BIG, BIG, too, and sometimes you scream and fight when you're angry. Big feelings can be hard to handle. It's my job as your mommy to help you learn to manage those big feelings, and to teach you what is okay and what is not okay. *(Guide the behavior)* It's okay to be angry! But it's not okay to disrupt everyone at school by screaming. Let's work on some ways you can express your big feelings without disrupting others."

By understanding and accepting his CoreSelf, I was able to lead with acceptance of Jordan as a boy who feels things deeply, knows what he wants, and never gives up. I let him know that I see and understand that about him, and that I appreciate and accept these things about him. After all, if channeled for the good, these can be amazing qualities! Then I took responsibility to teach him the proper behavior when he feels those big feelings. This is what is okay, and this is what is not okay. We will work on this together. I must be the leader in the situation and teach him how to manage his big feelings, how to deal with the disappointment of not getting everything he wants, and when/how to let go of things.

We consistently worked with Jordan in this manner. Each time he acted inappropriately, we tried to reinforce the message that we understood that he felt things deeply, and never gave up, and it was our job to teach him how to express himself appropriately. Blessedly, by the time he was five, his verbal skills were advanced enough that he could tell us how he was feeling rather than act out. He had also begun to internalize some of our limit setting, which allowed him to develop some self-control that continued to mature as he did.

Language

Language is a powerful tool. When speaking to or thinking about your child, it is paramount that you pay attention to the language you use.

Consider the difference that subtle shifts in language make:

LOW Activity
>   from lazy to relaxed
>   from lethargic to calm
>   from slow-moving to deliberate

HIGH Activity

>from hyper to dynamic
>
>from wild to vigorous
>
>from restless to energetic

LOW Adaptability

>from stubborn to predictable
>
>from rigid to consistent
>
>from shy to cautious

HIGH Adaptability

>from mercurial to flexible
>
>from chameleon-like to responsive
>
>from impulsive to open

LOW Distractibility

>from unresponsive to persistent
>
>from self-absorbed to focused
>
>from tuned out to tuned in

HIGH Distractibility

>from scatterbrained to responsive
>
>from space cadet to responsive to environment
>
>from unfocused to multi-tasker

LOW Ease with the Unfamiliar

>from scaredy-cat to cautious
>
>from withdrawn to observant
>
>from maladjusted to initially reserved

HIGH Ease with the Unfamiliar

>from reckless to receptive
>
>from risk taker to takes initiative
>
>from rushes headfirst to open to experiences

LOW Intensity

    from meek to mellow

    from mousy to reserved

    from unemotional to deliberate

HIGH Intensity

    from excitable to enthusiastic

    from melodramatic to exuberant

    from overly emotional to expressive

LOW Optimism

    from negative to realistic

    from pessimistic to thoughtful

    from antisocial to serious

HIGH Optimism

    from Pollyanna to hopeful

    from phony to sunny

    from being in denial to looking on the bright side

LOW Persistence

    from unreliable to multi-tasking

    from unfocused to responsive to environment

    from incompetent to needing support

HIGH Persistence

    from stubborn to persistent

    from tenacious to focused

    from pit bull to determined

LOW Regularity

    from erratic to variable schedule

    from disorganized to flexible

    from impulsive to adaptable

HIGH Regularity
> from rigid to consistent
>
> from inflexible to orderly
>
> from boring to predictable

LOW Sensory Reactivity
> from dull to self-contained
>
> from unnoticing to internal
>
> from oblivious to easygoing

HIGH Sensory Reactivity
> from finicky to tuned in
>
> from fussy to easily stimulated
>
> from picky to definite

Another Note on Language

At first, I would use the word "but" when I would explain things to Jordan ("I can see how much you're enjoying putting leaves in the clown trash can, *but* it's time for us to go…"). Especially with older children, try to avoid it; children can get desensitized to the word, waiting for you to lower the boom once they hear it. They learn to discount whatever comes before the "but" as the spoonful of sugar to help the medicine go down.

"At the same time," is a wonderful phrase to use, especially with older children. It reinforces the idea that several things can all be true at the same time. For instance, a child with a high activity level has trouble sitting still, and, at the same time, she needs to control her body during the sermon at church.

Now let's look at more examples of how separating a child's behavior from his CoreSelf helps parents lead with acceptance. Each of these three examples is a composite, based on real individuals, but fictionalized to illustrate common issues and children of different ages.

Nicholas Does Not Enjoy Sports

Nicholas, age nine, plays on the soccer and basketball teams, but only because he has to. His parents insist that he play a sport to be physically fit. Nicholas is intimidated by the body contact, so he hangs back and hopes no one will pass to him. His dad shouts at him from the sideline to be more aggressive. Nicholas wants to quit these team sports, but his dad won't let him.

1. *What is the hotspot?* Nicholas hates team sports and wants to quit. His parents insist he continue.

2. *What does that look like?* Nicholas and his dad have arguments before every game and he fights about going to practice. Nicholas says no one cares how he feels, and lashes out by telling his dad that he hates him.

3. *What role do CoreSelf traits play in the hotspot?*

	Lowest Level	Mid-Level	Highest Level
Activity	X		

> Low activity meant he did not enjoy intense physical exertion.

Adaptability N/A

Distractibility N/A

Ease with Unfamiliar N/A

Intensity	X		

> Low intensity meant he did not enjoy the competition and drama.

Optimism N/A

Distractibility N/A

Regularity N/A

Sensory Reactivity			X

> High sensory reactivity meant he was bothered by yelling and body contact.

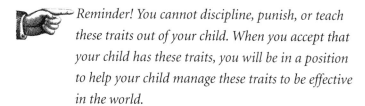 *Reminder! You cannot discipline, punish, or teach these traits out of your child. When you accept that your child has these traits, you will be in a position to help your child manage these traits to be effective in the world.*

4. *What role does learned behavior play in the hotspot?*
Nicholas has learned to express his feelings (anger, frustration, resentment) by verbally lashing out at his dad, because he knows it hurts his dad and he has not had any consequences for being disrespectful.

Leading with Acceptance:

I recommended that Nicholas' mom and dad look at whether his CoreSelf was a good fit with competitive team sports. As a low activity/low intensity/high sensory reactivity young man, Nicholas preferred activities such as hiking over loud, competitive action, and he could certainly get regular exercise by hiking on the weekends with his family and walking the dog briskly during the week. We agreed that, when his dad was ready, he would talk to Nicholas with a message similar to this:

> "Nicholas, you've been telling us for a long time that you don't like playing soccer and basketball, and we've been making you participate anyway. You know how important it is that we stay healthy and fit, and that's a good way to do it. But Mom and I realize that we could do a better job paying attention to who YOU are, and what YOU like. I guess I just wanted you to like what I like, but I see how unfair that is. You love to hike, and

we want to support you by hiking with you and getting fit together. It will be fun. At the same time, I am letting you know that you may not speak to me disrespectfully, no matter how angry you get. We'll be setting up consequences for you if it happens again, and Mom and I will work with you to find ways to express your frustration or your angry feelings without being disrespectful."

Understanding that forcing Nicholas to play competitive sports was not going to change his trait preferences helped his parents be flexible in their approach to his health and fitness. Communicating their understanding helped Nicholas feel accepted and gave him the incentive to take the lead in his own fitness.

Emilie Hurts Her Brother

Emilie is seven and has a three-year-old brother, Evan. Emilie has never warmed up to Evan, and is mean to him and makes fun of him. Evan idolizes Emilie and doesn't seem upset except when Emilie hits him, which she has started to do lately. He has now begun to hit her back.

1. *What is the hotspot?* Emilie is mean to her brother, and he tolerates it until she hits him, and then he fights back.

2. *What does that look like?* Emilie's parents wish the kids would get along but don't intervene until someone gets hurt. When Emilie hurts Evan, she is sent to timeout. If Evan hits back, she is told that she deserves it for being mean to him.

3. *What role do CoreSelf traits play in the hotspot?*

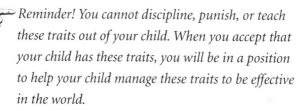

	Lowest Level	Mid-Level	Highest Level

Activity N/A

Adaptability _____ X _____

> Low adaptability meant she does not go with the flow.

Distractibility N/A

Ease with Unfamiliar N/A

Intensity _____ X ____

> High intensity meant she feels her feelings strongly.

Optimism ____ X _____

> Low optimism meant Emilie does not look on the bright side.

Distractibility N/A

Regularity N/A

Sensory Reactivity N/A

> *Reminder! You cannot discipline, punish, or teach these traits out of your child. When you accept that your child has these traits, you will be in a position to help your child manage these traits to be effective in the world.*

4. *What role does learned behavior play in the hotspot?* Emilie has learned to express her feelings about her brother by making fun of him, by being unkind, and by hitting him. All of these actions are learned responses to her normal feelings of anger, resentment, and frustration that stem from sibling rivalry.

Leading with Acceptance:

I recommended that Emilie's parents address Emilie's underlying feelings related to her sibling rivalry with Evan, which are normal and appropriate for an older sibling. In the context of Emilie's CoreSelf traits, we discussed the increased difficulty she might be having with adapting to all the changes that come with a sibling, as well as the high intensity level of her normal feelings of jealousy. Finally, her low optimism prevents her from letting it just roll off her back.

Emilie has learned to express herself through this filter of her CoreSelf, but hitting, being unkind, and making fun of her brother are learned behaviors that must be addressed. I recommended that her parents utilize leadership strategies to begin to guide Emilie to acceptable ways of expressing her feelings.

This dialogue was a suggested starting point to talk to Emilie:

"Emilie, Mom and I have decided that we need to do a better job of listening to you when you tell us how you're feeling. Sometimes you don't tell us in words; you tell us you're mad or frustrated by hitting Evan or acting unkindly. You're a young lady who feels things very deeply and when you're angry it can be hard. But hitting is never allowed, and Mom and I need to make sure we teach you the right way to get your feelings out without hurting others."

By separating out Emilie's behavior from her CoreSelf, her parents were able to acknowledge the legitimacy of her strong feelings regarding her brother, and identify what they needed to be doing as parent leaders.

Kayla Won't Do Her Chores

Kayla is fifteen, and the middle of three sisters. According to her parents, Kayla is the only one who does not pitch in around the house. The girls rotate their assigned chores monthly and receive their allowance in exchange for doing them. Kayla doesn't do the chores and usually doesn't get her allowance.

1.   *What is the hotspot?* Kayla does not listen to her parents or do her chores.

2.   *What does that look like?* Mom reminds Kayla to do her chores and Kayla says, "I will," but does not follow through. This continues until one or more of the following occur:

- Mom does the chore.
- Mom explodes and calls Kayla selfish.
- Kayla explodes and swears, screams, and slams doors.
- Kayla says she doesn't care about getting her allowance.

3. *What role do CoreSelf traits play in the hotspot?*

	Lowest Level	Mid-Level	Highest Level
Activity N/A			
Adaptability			X

> High adaptability meant Kayla doesn't thrive on routine.

Distractibility N/A

Ease with Unfamiliar N/A

| **Intensity** | | X | |

> High intensity meant she feels her feelings strongly.

Optimism N/A

Distractibility N/A

| **Regularity** | X | | |

> Low regularity meant Kayla did not have a predictable schedule.

| **Sensory Reactivity** | | | X |

> High sensory reactivity meant the smell of cleaning supplies triggered migraines.

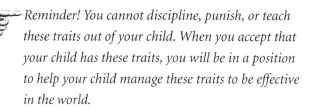

Reminder! You cannot discipline, punish, or teach these traits out of your child. When you accept that your child has these traits, you will be in a position to help your child manage these traits to be effective in the world.

4. *What role does learned behavior play in the hotspot?*
    Kayla had learned that there was little consequence to not doing her chores other than fights with her mother. The fights got her mom's attention, and, even though the attention was negative, it was still attention. She was not motivated by an allowance, since her dad gave her money whenever she asked him for it.

Leading with Acceptance:

I explained to Kayla's parents that, by nature, she was not into routine and did not thrive on schedules. Her high sensitivity to smell was making Kayla unwilling to do certain chores. I recommended that her parents become united in their leadership and adopt strategies from the leadership toolbox for parents, (see chapter 8) and that mom regularly connect with Kayla in a positive way to decrease her negative attention seeking.

Kayla's parents agreed to talk with her using dialogue similar to this:

"Kayla, we realize something about our relationship that we'd like to share with you. There's been so much yelling lately, and not much loving, and we want to turn that around. It seems like we fight about your chores all the time and everyone ends up angry. So, we're going to change the way we do things around here. We're going to stop paying allowance for doing your chores. You will get an allowance as a benefit of being a citizen of this family. At the same time, as a citizen of the family, you will be expected to contribute to the good of the family by doing your assigned chores. We will set up a system so that you know ahead of time what the consequences will be if you choose not to do your part, and we won't argue anymore about whether or not you do them. Instead of rotating chores, we want to be more understanding of your migraines and let you choose which ones won't be triggers. Finally, we realized that we haven't been spending much one-on-one time with you lately. We miss that special time together, so we're both going to make it a priority."

Kayla's parents made it easier for her to do her part for the family by adapting their requirements to her CoreSelf. Being parent leaders was a challenge, however, as both Mom and Dad did not have good role models for creating a cohesive family unit. With additional coaching, however, they learned some new strategies and found a good equilibrium for their family.

*

Can you see how accepting who these children are helped the parents address the problem behaviors? For some parents, just understanding their child's CoreSelf motivates them to make whatever changes are necessary so they don't make their child wrong for being who he is. These parents might say, "Okay, I see now how my son's talking back comes from his CoreSelf traits of persistence and intensity. I need to teach him how to express himself respectfully so we can have real discussions instead of screaming matches." Kayla's parents were able to do just that. Tuning in to and accepting the things about Kayla that were not going to change (especially her high sensory reactivity to smell) allowed them to connect with her and give her positive, loving attention. Just as important, they were able to see that more leadership was required on their part in order to hold everyone accountable for contributing to the family.

> For some parents, just understanding their
> child's CoreSelf motivates them to make
> whatever changes are necessary so they don't
> make their child wrong for being who he is.

Some parents have a more difficult time seeing their way clear to make necessary changes. Understanding their child's CoreSelf alone is not enough to motivate change. They have additional work to do before they will look at and take responsibility for the part they play in the family dynamics. Nicholas' parents and Emilie's parents went on to look at their roles in the family dynamics, described in the next chapter.

Let's face it: parenting is hard work. Maybe it's unrealistic to expect parents to have the motivation to look at themselves to understand their part of the equation. As a parent, you have needs, too, and all too often they are last on the list. Add to that the frustration of working hard and trying your best to do right by your child, and getting less than satisfying outcomes. When you put your heart and soul into parenting, it is helpful to feel like you're getting somewhere. You want to feel like a competent, caring parent who can positively influence your child's life.

As Cathy, a mom living in Derwood, Maryland, said, "Our differences with our kids have not posed any dramatic conflicts, but certainly there have been times when we just didn't understand how one of them could feel or do something a certain way, because neither my husband nor I would have felt or done the same way. And it is bewildering and sometimes hurtful when you feel like one of the persons you know best and love best in the entire world acts in a way you don't understand." It hurts and it is frustrating when you feel like you are constantly shot down.

*

When problems arise, a natural tendency is to try to fix the child. We don't naturally default to, "Hmmm, I wonder what's going on with me?" Instead, we ask ourselves, "How can I fix his behavior?" Sending a child to therapy or other experts can be an appropriate option, but can also be a cop-out when parents will not acknowledge that they play a role in their children's problems.

The next chapter will help make sure that the things you now understand about your child are things you understand about yourself as well.

Exercise

Choose a hotspot in your relationship with your child. Using the four-question analysis, separate CoreSelf traits from behavior. Does this process help you envision a leading with acceptance dialogue with your child?

What is the hotspot? _____

_____

_____

_____

_____

What does that look like? _____

_____

_____

_____

_____

*What role do CoreSelf traits play in the hotspot?*_____

_____

_____

_____

_____

What role does learned behavior play in the hotspot? _____

_____

_____

_____

_____

Chapter 7: Understanding Your CoreSelf and Your Behavior

If there is anything we wish to change in the child, we should first examine it and see whether it is not something that could better be changed in ourselves. — Carl Jung

Your child does not live in a vacuum. As we've discussed, how she behaves is the result of who influences her, and by her experiences in the world. In her earliest years, *you* provide the majority of her experience. Hotspots aren't due solely to your child. It's also about what *you* bring to the table. Once you can see how one plays off the other, you will be in a better position to understand the underlying issues that may be causing the conflict. Even if you are a parent who is not one to look inside yourself, this is a very doable and important next step.

Revisiting the CoreSelf traits, this time we will assess *your* CoreSelf. Not only will this help you better understand yourself, but it will also help you see how your CoreSelf fits with your child's. You may uncover some key reasons for ongoing conflicts with your child.[32]

Take a look at the nine traits of the CoreSelf below. Assess where you fit in as we go through the traits. In the exercises at the end of the chapter, you will compare your levels with those of your child.

ACTIVITY refers to the amount of physical movement a person engages in over time.

- LOW ACTIVITY: You may prefer to spend your weekend nights snug at home curled up with a book. You may enjoy meditating, or engaging in other relaxing activities. If your child has a high activity level, you might feel overwhelmed by her constant activity.
- HIGH ACTIVITY: You are a restless, high-energy person. You feel like you're wasting time if you aren't up and about. You get a lot done during the course of the day. If your child has a low activity level, you might view him as lazy.

ADAPTABILITY refers to the flexibility or resistance a person has to changes in routines, plans, and their environment.

- LOW ADAPTABILITY: You thrive on routine. You don't wonder how things might be better, and have no motivation to change things you don't have to. If your child is highly adaptable, you might be uncomfortable with his exploration, wishing he could stick to one thing.
- HIGH ADAPTABILITY: You don't mind changes to your routine, and in fact enjoy change, viewing it as an adventure. You are tolerant of others and go with the flow. If your child has low adaptability, you might resent her unwillingness to try new things.

DISTRACTIBILITY is how well a person can tune out interruptions and outside stimuli.

- LOW DISTRACTIBILITY: You've always been able to focus on the task at hand, even in a noisy environment. If your child is highly distractible, you might not understand her need to keep her bedroom door shut in order to get her homework done.

- HIGH DISTRACTIBILITY: You shift your focus to whatever is in front of you. Sometimes you wonder what you did all day. If your child has low distractibility, you might insist that he not listen to music while he studies, even though he says it helps him focus.

EASE WITH THE UNFAMILIAR refers to how bold or hesitant a person's initial reaction is to new people, places, foods and other stimuli.

- LOW EASE WITH THE UNFAMILIAR: You've always taken a while to warm up to new people and experiences. You are cautious about trying new foods or activities. If your child has high ease with the unfamiliar, you might envy his relaxed approach.

- HIGH EASE WITH THE UNFAMILIAR: You've always been eager to meet and talk to new people. If your child has low ease with the unfamiliar, you might worry that he is too shy or withdrawn and won't have friends.

INTENSITY is the energy level of a person's responses, irrespective of whether the response is positive or negative.

- LOW INTENSITY: People comment on how chilled and mellow you are. When you are angry about something, you do not raise your voice. If your child has high intensity, you might be uncomfortable with her loud outbursts.

- HIGH INTENSITY: You've always had strong opinions, and you don't have any problems expressing them. Whether you are upset or feeling great, people can tell. If your child has low intensity, you might have trouble figuring out what kind of mood she's in and how she feels.

OPTIMISM refers to the general pattern of outlook on life.

- LOW OPTIMISM: You are what others call serious. You like to be prepared for any contingency, and are likely to plan your actions. You may have a pessimistic view of life. In humor, you tend to be dry and ironic. If your child has high optimism, his cheeriness might grate on you.
- HIGH OPTIMISM: You are bubbly and cheerful. You tend to wake up every morning in a good mood ready to take on the day. If your child has low optimism, his "glass half empty" approach might annoy you.

PERSISTENCE refers to a person's stick-to-it-iveness when faced with challenges.

- LOW PERSISTENCE: You tend to give up easily, especially on tasks that don't seem that important to you. You don't like long-term projects. If your child has high persistence, you might envy her string of accomplishments.
- HIGH PERSISTENCE: You are steadfast and determined when it comes to accomplishing whatever you set out to do. If your child has low persistence, you might be-

lieve that she doesn't care about doing well.

REGULARITY refers to the predictability of a person's eating, sleeping, and eliminating.

- LOW REGULARITY: You don't need to follow a set routine and prefer to have variation in your days. You don't mind waking up and discovering throughout the day how it unfolds. If your child is highly regular, you might feel she is too set in her ways.

- HIGH REGULARITY: You are a devoted disciple to routine. You wake up at the same time each day, and prefer a set schedule. If your child has low regularity, you might consider her undisciplined.

SENSORY REACTIVITY refers to the level at which a person ignores or is bothered by external stimuli such as sounds, light, temperature, textures, and tastes.

- LOW SENSORY REACTIVITY: You are not bothered by loud noises or strange smells that waft into your environment. If your child has high sensory reactivity and can't tolerate many kinds of clothing, you might think he is too finicky.

- HIGH SENSORY REACTIVITY: You can't eat any foods with a mushy texture or be in a place where the smell is strange or foreign to you. Certain clothes bug you. If your child has low sensory reactivity, you might wish you felt more at ease, like him.

By comparing your CoreSelf trait levels with your child's, you can start to identify possible reasons for the hotspots in your relationship.

How Does Your CoreSelf Align with Your Child's?

How does looking at the alignment of your CoreSelf traits with your child's help us identify reasons for hotspots? Because problems can arise when there are either:

- significant differences in trait level(s), or
- strong similarities in trait level(s)

Just as you can't change your child's innate preferences, neither can you change yours. But knowledge is power, and by comparing your CoreSelf trait levels with your child's, you can start to identify possible reasons for the hotspots in your relationship. These hotspots are blocks to closeness and connection, and identifying the reasons can help you defuse them.

Jacky Howell, the child educator we met in Chapter 4, who now runs workshops for early childhood educators, parents, and families in the Washington, D.C. metropolitan area, agrees that it takes an understanding of who you are, combined with an understanding of who your child is: "I think it is a challenge for parents. It's the story you tell of active city parents who have a laid-back country child, and laid-back parents who have an active city child. I think a lot of times, parents think children will change to their way of being, rather than accommodate and work with who their children are."

In leading with acceptance, we accept our children's Core-Selves, and at the same time hold them accountable to behave properly. The same is true for us as parents. We don't try to change who we are, but we know that we can always change our behavior. It's important that we take responsibility for how we behave, because it's through our behavior that our children know us. It's how we show up as parents.

Significant Differences in Trait Levels: Mismatches

In the description of the nine traits discussed previously, we looked at some more examples of these mismatches. Looking a bit deeper, we can see how these simple temperament issues can lead to ongoing problems. Your low persistence child doesn't take after you, the tenacious problem solver? He's lazy. Your high activity preschool daughter is considered hyper because she doesn't enjoy quiet afternoons reading books with you. Your low optimism daughter brings the family down and you nickname her "Debbie Downer."

But, if you realize that you were born with high optimism (meaning you always wake up happy and see the good in a situation), and your son was born with low optimism, his sarcastic and skeptical approach to life might not bother you as much. You realize that he's not simply acting that way; it's part of his nature. Instead of criticizing him for his negativity, you can help him see, without judgment or blame, that other people look at things differently, and the effect his outlook has on himself and others.

For the children we met in the previous chapter, significant differences in trait levels led to hotspots with their parents. Let's take a look at how the parents' CoreSelves contributed to the hotspots in those relationships. Without ever really thinking about it, Nicholas' dad had expected his son to be like him. However, when he looked at his own CoreSelf traits and compared them to his son's, he became aware of the big differences between himself and his son in activity level, intensity, and sensory reactivity. Dad thrived on the rough and tumble, but his son hated it. When Dad realized that Nicholas was born this way and no amount of team sports would "bring him around," the decision to let Nicholas stop playing team sports was easy to make.

Emilie's parents looked at their own CoreSelf traits in order to understand the hotspot around Emilie's treatment of Evan. Both parents were high in adaptability and low in intensity, the opposite of Emilie in those traits. That meant that they were able to let things roll off their backs and were quite tolerant of others. Emilie's low adaptability and high intensity meant she didn't fare well with the unpredictability of a toddler brother and took everything to heart. Once her parents realized that these CoreSelf traits were inborn, they let go of the notion that Emilie was intentionally being difficult and helped her manage her strong feelings.

Kayla's parents were able to identify her high sensory re-activity as a contributing factor in their conflict, and stopped brushing aside Kayla's complaints.

*

Recently, I listened to a dear friend, Jill, vent about the frustration she felt because her ten-year-old daughter would not co-operate and make her bed. Every day, Jill would see the unmade bed and get angry that Morgan didn't take pride in keeping her room orderly and neat. I asked her to evaluate Morgan's levels of regularity and adaptability. As we talked, it was as if a light bulb went off in her head. "She doesn't care about making her bed because routine and order are not important to her," she exclaimed, as if making a profound new discovery. And it *was* a profound discovery for her, because she now saw clearly that her expectation that her daughter care about having a neat room was causing the problem, not helping to solve it.

Jill talked to Morgan about her newfound insight. The conversation went something like this:

"You know how I'm constantly on your case about making the bed? I realized something important about that."

Morgan looked up from her texting.

"I know it sounds simple," Jill continued, "but I realized that it's not important to *you* to have an orderly environment. It doesn't bother you, so why would I expect you to *want* to make your bed? I'm the one who is bothered when the bed is unmade."

This shift, away from blaming her daughter for being "a slob" helped them work together to come up with a compromise that worked for both of them. They agreed to simplify the bed-making with just a duvet that Morgan could pull up and be done. Morgan wanted assurance that if she made the effort, her mom would not criticize the job she did or redo it altogether. Last I heard, they appreciated the closeness they felt when they were able to laugh at their own quirks.

The parents described above were able to shift their thinking and defuse their hotspots once they become consciously aware of the mismatch in CoreSelf traits. Realizing that they were making their children wrong for being who they are was the motivation they needed to make the changes. Unfortunately, that's not always the case. Some parents need a more dramatic wake-up call.

Mismatches Can Lead to Unrealistic and Damaging Expectations

Robert Brooks, PhD, specializes in resilience, motivation, and family relationships. He believes that many of the stresses in parent-child relationships come from expectations parents give their children that they are unable to meet, given their unique temperaments. He wrote poignantly of a six-year-old girl he saw in his office:

> [E]very day after school her mother asked, "Did you speak to other kids today?" While this question was obviously based on mother's anxiety that her daughter be more outgoing, what mother was unaware of was the role that inborn temperament played in her daughter's behavior and how this daily question was intensifying her daughter's distress. Her daughter would have given anything to feel at ease greeting others but was unable to do so given her intense anxiety. In the school environment, children who are shy often sit in terror at the thought of being called upon to answer a question or to read aloud.[33]

When I read this, my first reaction was that there was a mismatch in the trait of ease with the unfamiliar. Mom was probably socially outgoing and high in this trait, and expected her daughter to be like her. It's natural, after all, to envision the Child You Want to be just like you, and especially in a way that is as highly valued in our culture as being outgoing. Here, the mother pushed her daughter to speak to the other kids, as if this would transform her daughter into the child she wanted. She acted as if the child she wanted was hidden inside her daughter, and, with enough prodding, the better version would emerge, socially at ease and popular. Unfortunately, her actions gave her daughter the message that who she was and how she was (low in ease with the unfamiliar) was wrong. But, not to worry, with Mom's help, she could be fixed. As a result, her daughter's discomfort was exacerbated and her conflict intensified.

In *Quiet: The Power of Introverts in a World That Can't Stop*

Talking, author Susan Cain says, "If you're an introvert, you also know that the bias against quiet can cause deep psychic pain. As a child you might have overheard your parents apologize for your shyness. Or at school you might have been prodded to come "out of your shell" — that noxious expression which fails to appreciate that some animals naturally carry shelter everywhere they go, and some humans are just the same."[33]

Consider another possibility, however, for Dr. Brooks' scenario: that mom might have wanted to spare her daughter some pain she herself had endured as a child, in which case there was not a mismatch, but rather a strong similarity between mother and daughter. We address strong similarities and the sometimes unexpected difficulties they can create next.

The Double-Edged Sword: Strong Similarities in Trait Levels

What parent wouldn't want a "mini-me"? At least a mini-me of the best parts of me — that's the Child You Want! Don't we all know someone who has a child who seems exactly like them? They look alike, walk alike, talk alike, and think alike. When parent and child are this much alike, they will have strong similarities in their level of many of the nine traits.

It can be a beautiful thing when parent and child just "get" each other implicitly. But it can be a double-edged sword. When parent and child are alike in certain traits, it can lead to ongoing conflict. For example, if parent and child are both highly persistent, they might butt heads repeatedly. Look also at the trait of intensity. If both mother and daughter have high intensity, normal clashes may escalate quickly and dangerously, especially if the parent does not take charge and de-escalate the situation. These types of hotspots can be spotted using the nine traits assessment, and parents can defuse them by being leaders who craft compromises that allow everyone to be who they are. This is discussed in Chapter 8.

When parent and child are alike in certain traits, it can lead to ongoing conflict.

But it's not always as simple as just pointing out the similarity. Sometimes, similarities in CoreSelf traits can lead to emotional triggers in the parent. What if parent and child are very much alike, but in ways that the parent is not happy about? We have discussed how we learn to tuck away pieces of ourselves that are not accepted by our parents or primary caregivers. What if your child is just like you in this way? You'll be triggered by the behavior of your child who is like you in this way. It will bring up feelings of shame. And what makes this even more challenging is that it's often not conscious.

Remember how I described Jordan as an infant? He was a mini-me in intensity and persistence, and this similarity could have led to some major problems. Not just because two intense and persistent people are bound to have some strong clashes: it went deeper than that. Jordan's personality echoed my own, but it echoed parts of my personality that I had tried to tuck away in order to earn my mother's approval. My own persistence and intensity had been difficult for her to handle. Whether she was triggered by my temperament or just exhausted by my tenaciousness, I felt rejected for my big, bold, loud, insistent self. I tried to tuck away this (very fundamental) part of who I was, by attempting to "be like the others." Unbeknownst to my conscious self, I tried to avoid situations where my strong personality might have emerged (and been an asset!), such as leadership, performing, or debate. When I spoke up in groups without holding back first and measuring my response, I was invariably filled with remorse about having been too insistent, too forceful, too loud. Too me.

Imagine now having a baby with those same temperament traits. I was triggered. I didn't want to face my own shame and couldn't possibly have been an accepting mother to my beautiful son had I not looked inside myself. Without my epiphany, what chance would Jordan have had to grow up comfortable in his own bold, tenacious skin? Not much of a chance, if I had rejected him for who he was or tried desperately to get him to be different so I wouldn't have to feel uncomfortable. With his mother acting out her own issues through him, he would most likely have joined in a sad intergenerational legacy of unconscious self-hatred.

If we learn to accept even the parts of ourselves we deem negative, we'll better accept others who exhibit these characteristics. What bothers us most is actually within us. When parents are triggered by a child who reminds them of something they don't wish to acknowledge in themselves, it's natural to try to control the child. There's a reason that stuff got tucked away in the first place! It felt horrible. Of course, the reason has nothing to do with the child and perhaps nothing to do with today. But, if we don't deal with our tucked away pain, we unwittingly set up the damaging expectation, "Don't be who you are." We try to force our kids to play along with us. It's as if we're saying, "I need you to do this for me." What the child hears is, "Don't be who you are," "My needs are more important than yours," and "I don't have faith in who you are."

Bella, a sixteen-year-old high school sophomore, described her relationship with her father and it reminded me of the danger when a parent has unresolved issues. I suspected that he hasn't come to terms with his own mistakes, and got triggered when he sensed weakness or vulnerability in his kids. Bella said:

> "My sister and I live with my dad. He made so many bad decisions in his life growing up. But he got his act together and has made something of himself, I have to give him credit for that. The problem, though, is because he made so many mistakes, he puts so much pressure on us to do things "right" — the first time. Which means listening to him because he's "always right." He can't stand to hear anything from me that shows any weakness or uncertainty. He's just so afraid I'll mess up, like he did. He doesn't give me any credit for having good judgment or common sense. Most adults comment on how level-headed and mature I am. But my own father sees me so differently! Like I'm just waiting to screw up if he gives up control of me — even for five seconds. Plus, he just focuses on negatives all the time. When I'm around him, it feels like I'm just one big disappointment. He doesn't see any of my good qualities. It's a joke to say he doesn't accept me for who I am. How can I even know who I am when he won't let me make my own choices and learn from my mistakes? When I finally move out for college, I'll be able to do that. But for now, I just play his little game so I don't make him angry."

Bella cannot be honest with her father; instead, she "play[s] his little game." Although her situation might seem extreme, this is the root of why many teens don't talk to their parents about what's going on in their lives. Whether their parents insist on solving their problems, punish them for not being perfect, or cannot be emotionally present with the child's reality, these children do not show their parents who they are. As Bella so poignantly expresses, "How can I even know who I am when he won't let me make my own choices and learn from my mistakes?"

Madeline Levine recently wrote, "Our greatest act of love is to let our children know that we support their growth and development over our own understandable, but ultimately unhelpful, desire to control all aspects of their lives."[35]

A particularly damaging thing about the Child You Want is that we don't see ourselves as separate from our child. It's a fantasy designed to heal us, to make us whole.

What about the parent with the perfect mini-me child? Hotspots are not always as clear cut. These kids are not criticized as much as kids who are unlike or who trigger unpleasant feelings in their parents. Since hotspots tend to surface later, these kids might not act out when they're young.

With these "perfect" kids, over-identification by the parents is a real danger, leading to difficulty in seeing the whole of who the child is. But they are often not accepted for who they are. They are so similar to the Child You Want, your perfect child! For instance, Dad is a terrific athlete and was the varsity quarterback in high school. If his son is also a jock, Dad may have trouble seeing his son as a separate person. Levine also wrote, "The first creative act of parenting is to understand that you and your child are two different people."[35]

A particularly damaging thing about the Child You Want is that we don't see ourselves as separate from our child. The Child You Want is an extension of us. It's a fantasy designed to heal us, to make us whole. It's a reflection of who we want to be. There is no need to "see" the Child You Want as separate from us. This is not true of the Child You've Got. This is a living person. We may have given birth to this person, we may have provided half this person's genetic makeup, we may be responsible for the well-being of this person for eighteen years, but we are not this person and this person is not us. "Of course we're not the same person," you say. "I don't think that!" Well, too many parents blur that line. It's often due to unacknowledged issues, feelings, or needs of the parent. And it leads to harmful expectations of who the child needs to be, which do not respect that the child has his own CoreSelf that must be respected.

> "Nothing has a stronger influence psychologically on their environment and especially on their children than the unlived life of the parent." — Carl Jung

"Hang your fading hopes and dreams on your children's high-school teams!"

An obvious example of not seeing the Child You've Got as a separate person is when the child's life becomes a vehicle for parents to relive the glory of their own youth. Often, these kids feel invisible, existing only to make their parents happy, while feeling powerless and frustrated in their desire to make their own decisions.

> "Allow children to be happy in their way,
> for what better way will they find?" — Samuel Johnson

Teenager Kailey shared how her mother over-identified with her daughter's goals, to a point where Kailey felt like her voice was lost:

> "I've loved gymnastics since I was in preschool, have lots of talent, and love my coach and teammates. We're like family. The problem is with my mom. She was a gymnast growing up and she competed in the Olympics. She has told me every single day for my whole life that I'll make the Olympic team. Guess what? I don't even want to compete in the Olympics! It's not like I could just soak in the experiences and enjoy them all. She'd be putting so much pressure on me to medal it'd be a freaking nightmare! Everything is on gymnastics and my making the Olympic team. She tries to make it like it's all about me. Guess what? It's not! It's 100 percent about her — but she doesn't see it."

Do you remember the powerful fantasies we have of who we wish our children will become? This is an example of a fantasy of a Child You Want that has taken over a mother-daughter relationship.

Are You Too Invested in Your Child's Success?

Parents who make top achievement a priority for their children often create a situation where the child needs to accomplish in order to earn the parent's love. Children get on a treadmill that's difficult to get off, fearing abandonment for not living up to their parents' expectations. The question is: why is achievement so important for some of these parents?

Author and mother Amy Chua, aka "Tiger Mother," has become infamous for her book *The Battle Hymn of the Tiger Mother*, where she describes her harsh methods for turning her children into prodigies, something that she, being a Chinese-American mother, justified as part of the Chinese culture. In her view, rigid expectations are necessary in order to mold your children into who you want them to be. Interestingly, her methods worked well with her first child, whose CoreSelf was compliant, calm, contemplative, and eager to please. Yet, it's no surprise that her younger daughter rebelled against her mother's oppressive expectations, as her CoreSelf was quite different: hot-tempered, warrior-like, and sharp-tongued. Mom ultimately eased up on this younger daughter, but there were years of battles before peace. One can see why this book shocked so many readers; it purports that fulfilling the benchmarks a parent deems acceptable is the way to raise a child. In reality, fulfilling these rigid expectations ultimately only pleases one person: the parent.

I was in my second year of law school when I woke up from what I call my "trance of accomplishment." Doing well academically had been a way to please my mother, and I realized that I was where I was in the hope that she would turn to me and say, "Look at you! You're amazing!" I was no more invested in being a lawyer than I would have been in something else, except that I thought it might impress her. How different my life would have been if I hadn't grown up chasing her approval by being what I thought she wanted me to be. Then again, I was in my early twenties when I awoke to the absurdity of my path and changed my course, for which I feel quite fortunate. Interestingly, my mother wasn't the one who was overly invested in my success — I was overly invested in my success as a way to be liked by her.

Many parents, however, do seem to be invested in their children's success as a way to validate themselves. Jennifer Little, who spoke in Chapter 2 of parents' ego interests in their children, points out the dangers inherent when they see the child's degree of success in the world as a reflection of their character or abilities as a parent.

I put responsibility squarely on the shoulders of parents to take the lead and do what it takes to make the emotional shifts necessary to raise the Child They've Got — not the One They Want.

The movie *Race to Nowhere* highlights the dark side of America's over-achievement culture; notably, the damage stemming from pressuring students to excel in all areas. It has spawned a social action movement both to reform America's educational system and to reclaim healthy childhoods that encourage meaningful learning.

Challenge Success,[37] a project developed by Stanford University's School of Education, also introduces game-changing ideas on what success means for kids. In redefining success,

Challenge Success shows how practical measures empower success in broader ways. *Race to Nowhere* and Challenge Success offer valuable suggestions on how parents can support their children by not buying into the culture of over-achievement.

I take it a step further and point out how parents' expectations affect their children's pressure-cooker environments and personal development. In addition, I put responsibility squarely on the shoulders of parents to take the lead and do what it takes to make the emotional shifts necessary to raise the Child They've Got — not the one they want. In this way, they can meet their children's fundamental need for acceptance and help them become the best version of who they are.

Family psychologist, *Psychology Today* blogger, and author Carl Pickhardt wrote, "Where a child's high achievement becomes a paramount parenting priority, and censure follows any degree of failure, the child can end up feeling treated more like a "human doer" than a human *being*, valued as a performer more than a person, having to earn parental love rather than having it guaranteed."[38] The difference between viewing your child as a human doer rather than a human being is profound. Perhaps one of the greatest gifts a parent can give his or her child is the opportunity to freely express who he is — to *be*, rather than act in ways that will please the parent in the short term.

Do What It Takes to Make the Emotional Shifts

For parents who resist looking at themselves, I understand their reluctance. Introspection can be hard for those who are not used to it, but it's doable. Just by acknowledging that you are part of the equation is a powerful first step. Remember, you come to parenting carrying your own experience of growing up. The beliefs you bring to your family were set in motion by your relationship with your own parents, and by their relationship with their parents, and so on. It's not about something *you've* done or didn't do. You already know how my relationship with Jordan echoed my mother's relationship with me. Now it's your turn to gain knowledge and empower yourself in your relationship with your child.

In order to make a shift toward acceptance of who your child is, you might need to feel pain that you would rather not feel. What is encouraging is that many parents will do for their children what they would not necessarily do for themselves. Like me during my epiphany, they would walk through fire rather than inflict pain on their child. Their deep love for their child gives them the strength to face buried pain. The beauty is that the buried pain becomes buried treasure, ready to transform your relationship with yourself, your children, and possibly your parents.

The beauty is that the buried pain becomes buried treasure, ready to transform your relationship with yourself, your children, and possibly your parents.

Parents sometimes tell me that making changes in order to accept who their children are, "is soooooo hard!"

I ask them, "How hard is a troubled, distant relationship with your child? How hard will it be to be alienated from your child and their family?" Don't sweep the challenge under the rug, because lack of acceptance will wound your child's heart and soul in a way that will lead to a lifetime of struggle between you. What are you willing to do to prevent that from happening?

Make no mistake — everyone has a way to access his or her suppressed pain. No matter how foreign the idea that looking inside yourself is a good thing to do, anyone who has the desire to make a change can find a way to do so.

ARE YOU WILLING? by Ralph Marston[39]

Forget the excuses, let go of the shoulds, move beyond the if onlys and ask yourself this one question. Are you willing or are you not?

All the many things that go into any achievement can be reduced to one clear and simple factor. And that is — are you willing?

When you are willing to do what it takes, you'll find a way. When you are willing, though circumstances conspire against you, you'll get it done anyway. When you're truly willing, the problems have a way of being transformed into opportunities. When you're really willing, the disappointments have a way of making you even more determined.

If you're willing, that's great — go for it with everything you have. Yet, if you're not willing, there's still a way to become so.

Somewhere, somehow, there is something that will inspire and engage you fully. Connect yourself with it and suddenly you'll be willing, willing to do whatever it takes.

What might seem too dark, too shameful, too treacherous is just waiting to be addressed and let go of. Don't fear giving expression to the negative by voicing it. You're giving it a more powerful expression by suppressing it. Someone once said the enemy of shame is disclosure. Brené Brown is a *New York Times* bestselling author and an expert on shame. She wrote, "If we can share our story with someone who responds with empathy and understanding, shame can't survive."[40] The energy required to carry buried pain is enormous. A common discovery is that, when parents find the motivation to look at their unresolved issues, it's easier than carrying the pain around with them.

> No matter how foreign the idea
> that looking inside yourself is a good thing
> to do, anyone who has the desire to make a
> change can find a way to do so.

The earlier in your parenting experience you start, the easier it will be to make the emotional shifts and let go of your expectations. There is a saying that expectations are resentments under construction, and I believe this to be true. Mind you, we're talking about expectations about who your child must be, not expectations about how your child should behave. Do you want resentments to build or do you want to make the shifts now?

One father from Colorado, who used to be a practicing psychotherapist, urges parents to unearth all of their issues *before* committing to parenthood. Sometimes that might require counseling. He says that before he and his wife became parents, they embarked on a journey to ensure they were completely, emotionally prepared. The goal? To completely understand their own gifts and deficits in order to be the best teachers, supporters, and fellow human beings to their kids. "We had to learn how to climb the Himalayas together," he explains. "We have to learn to work through all of our stuff, all of our junk. By the time we had kids and got married, we were ready. We had the strong dynamic." He also explained that people who aren't emotionally ready need to take a long, hard look at their core issues before plunging into parenthood. "If you don't, this kid from three or four years old on will remember everything. If you want to sit across from your kid and deal with hellfire twenty years later — something that happened to me and my parents — that's no fun. First and foremost, work on yourself, work on your issues."

Whether you do it before you have children, or while you're raising them, tune in enough to get the assistance you need to accept the Child You've Got.

Seeing Where You Need Extra Help

It's important to remember that, throughout your child's life, you *will* make mistakes. It's natural and part of the process. But, there are tools you can use to better educate yourself on how you can best situate yourself to give the most you can to your child.

For those who are open to it, individual psychotherapy can be life changing. It doesn't have to be years of work. A course of therapy aimed at a particular issue can do wonders for your relationship with your child. Family therapy is useful for any family that is willing. Sometimes you'll uncover things only when everyone is talking together.

Another approach is coaching, which can be very effective in helping people make changes in their lives. Sometimes parents who are resistant to the idea of therapy are willing to be coached.

Consider workshops as well. Jacky Howell, the education expert we heard from earlier in this chapter, says that workshops where *both* parent and teacher are present can be an invaluable learning experience. Many parents don't fully grasp that, often, a child interacts totally differently from how she may act in the comfort of her own home. "Today, parents feel pressure that, 'My child should be knowing this,' or 'My child should be learning these things.' Parents do feel a certain pressure that their child needs to be doing well or better, but often they don't even know what 'well' is. I give many workshops on what it means to be a one-year-old, on what four-year-olds are capable of, or on what kids should be able to do by five years old. I've found that some families just don't know. I end up telling them, 'Really, there's nothing wrong with your child, he's being four. This is how they see things. This is why they have so many questions.'"

Jacky spoke of her mom, who said that, years ago, it was easier for a parent to feel informed because she could go out in the yard and talk to other moms. Today, it's not like that; instead, parents turn more often to early childhood programs, or a preschool classroom for information.

The important thing is to tune in to your relationship with your child, and be open to looking at your role as well as your child's. Consider Laurie, a social worker and gregarious mom to introverted Emily, who shared her journey in not only understanding her child, but also connecting with her. She said, "I worried that I had failed as a parent and as a social worker, somehow not creating a safe enough world for her to speak up despite my every attempt to be a nurturing and loving parent. One friend even said to me, 'Well, Laurie, if you'd just shut up, she might talk to you.' I tried that one whole weekend to no avail! Another friend suggested that my 'über-extroverted self' might be intimidating Emily and her way of dealing with it was to shut herself down...which made her feel more powerful. Ouch. I felt like a pushy, hyper, overly talkative harpy."

As time went on, however, Laurie became a sponge for any knowledge she could use to understand her daughter. She "enlisted" the help of teachers, friends, and experts. "Early on, Emily's kindergarten teachers started helping me recognize that the basic differences between introverts and extroverts did not represent the differences between superior and inferior people. They just represented differences, each with their own set of skills and contributions to make. They were so enthusiastic about her strengths, and so confident that she would be successful in her future, that some of my fears and frustrations were lessened. I took it upon myself to learn more about introverts and started realizing a whole lot of misconceptions I had had."

Once *you* are confident, healthy, stable, and open, you are the best tool in your child's arsenal for his happiness and success.

Everyone who is willing has a path toward understanding themselves. I've had therapy, which has been invaluable. Meditation has allowed me to understand much about myself and how I operate in the world. But the one unexpected tool for self-discovery has been the 5Rhythms[41] method of conscious dance, because it got me "into my body." Over-thinkers like me can happily analyze and intellectualize issues ad nauseum. On the contrary, feeling the emotions in my body allows me to experience them physically and, often, to work them out on the dance floor. Once I discovered how well I responded to this "moving meditation," my self-awareness skyrocketed. Everyone's path is different, and what works for me is not necessarily what will work for you. The important thing to remember is that, if you are willing to look inside, there is a path for you toward your truth.

Once *you* are confident, healthy, stable, and open, you are the best tool in your child's arsenal for his happiness and success. Small insights can make a big difference. Taking even the first step with your child, like telling an older child that you're going to take a look at your expectations and work on them, can be profoundly healing. Do it today.

Exercise

On the chart from Chapter 5, use an *0* to mark your level of each trait, and compare it to your child's level.

Where are there significant differences between you and your child? Did any of the results surprise you?

Where are there strong similarities between you and your child? Did any of the results surprise you?

Part III
Lead the Child You've Got
with Acceptance

Coupling acceptance with leadership is the next and final step to providing a nurturing, positive, strengthening environment so your child can become the best version of who she is. Having accepted the Child You've Got, you are poised for powerful leadership that creates true influence.

It's now easier to understand what a "successful parent" looks like. How about:

Success as a parent is ensuring my child's lifelong well-being by helping her become the best version of who she is. With that understanding, my first task is to understand and accept who she is. Then, while accepting and honoring her CoreSelf, I lead our family to shape her character and teach her proper behavior so she can be effective in the community and the world. I do not impose my idea of success on her; instead, by accepting her as she is, I empower her to get to know and like herself, become comfortable in her own skin, and discover her own path.

In this way, she is continually becoming the best version of who she is.

Part III will show you how to be the leader you need to be while using acceptance as your starting point, as well as making the case that everyone thrives when parents lead with acceptance.

Chapter 8: Being the Leader Who Guides Your Child

"I've found what makes children happy doesn't always prepare them to be courageous, engaged adults." — Brené Brown

You've done the work to accept the Child You've Got. Congratulations! You're now at the correct starting point. That's right — the starting point. You've created the foundation and have a strong parent-child connection brought about by your loving acceptance. Now, your job is to shepherd your child through the growing up years. These are the trenches of parenting, where you walk the walk, day in and day out. But, hold on, it's not what you might be thinking — the hamster wheel we discussed, where you wake up every morning facing the same problems, or waiting for the other shoe to drop. No. When you lead with acceptance, it's not a thankless grind; it's a gratifying journey as you guide your child to be the best version of who she is.

Why Acceptance Must Be Coupled with Leadership

You've no doubt caught on that the phrase "lead with acceptance" has a double meaning. You start your parenting by accepting the Child You've Got, so you are leading with acceptance. Now, you're going to couple that acceptance with leadership, because this is how you will guide your child to become the best version of who he is.

In leading with acceptance, we make sure that every child is given license to shine their own unique light, while at the same time teaching them that they are part of something bigger than themselves. Wendy Mogel, whom we heard from in previous chapters, describes some beautiful Hasidic wisdom about understanding our place in the world.

"Keep two pieces of paper in your pockets at all times. On one write, 'I am a speck of dust.' On the other, 'The world was created for me.'"[42]

Leaders understand and accept their child's CoreSelves, and also know how to make firm decisions in his best interest — even in difficult situations.

Leading with acceptance brings this wisdom to our modern lives, by making sure that our children know that they are special, but no more special than anyone else. This sets children up for success, because they have a realistic picture of who they are and their place in the world. It takes leadership to teach this lesson.

When parents are leaders, they give their children the security of knowing that they are committed to raising them right. Leaders understand and accept their child's CoreSelves, and also know how to make firm decisions in his best interest — even in difficult situations. Being present and listening when children are experiencing strong emotions, for instance, is crucial in creating a strong parent-child connection. You are looking out for his long-term best interest, which takes both his specialness and his not-so-specialness into account. It's work. It's the trenches. But it's not the hamster wheel. And, without this commitment, you risk getting caught up in one of the twin troubling situations described below.

Troubling Situation #1: Acceptance without Leadership

What happens when parents accept their children, but fail to provide the leadership to teach them how to behave in the world? Acceptance without leadership can create adults who, in many ways, do not function as healthy members of society. As Naomi Aldort, author of *Raising Our Children, Raising Ourselves,* says, "Children experience love easily when they can rely on clear parental guidance…When we give clear guidance the child can count on, she leans against the walls we provide and is free to explore and to grow."[43] This makes perfect sense, doesn't it? Think about reality television stars or celebrities, who seem to crave drama or a platform for their vices, for instance. Are these people the best versions of who they are? Arguably, no, they are not. While they happily show who they are to the world and may be completely accepted by their parents — gifts, deficits, and all — they often lack even a minimum of discernment and social grace. Have you ever asked yourself, "Who taught them while they were growing up?"

A parent who accepts but does not lead
can create a situation where the child takes
advantage of rules, grows up without learning
respect, and can ultimately enter the
adult world unprepared.

Children first learn what is expected of them at home. This is the area where parents have enormous influence. Not where you think you do — in who your child is — but in the teaching of proper behavior, values, and morals. *Parents* are the ones who teach children to be polite (such as saying please and thank you appropriately), practice table manners, look people in the eye when speaking to them, and finish chores before playtime. We teach our children about making choices and being responsible. Children learn what is acceptable conduct and what is not through *us*. We teach them our values and our morals. We build the foundation. As they move out into the world, they learn what is expected of them at school, in their peer groups, at work, and later as they journey through life as part of society. This is why initial parental leadership is pivotal.

A parent who accepts but does not lead can create a situation where the child takes advantage of rules, grows up without learning respect, and can ultimately enter the adult world unprepared to be effective in interactions with others.

Jerry, a retired teacher and counselor whom we met earlier in this book, shared his observations of what happens when a child doesn't have the firm rules or structures he believes a parent should provide. "Kids need to know that someone is in charge and it's not them," he related. "Kids will be angry and test limits, but I've seen kids really start to panic when the parents step back from that important leadership role. Then, it's so easy for these kids to make bad choices."

Jerry shared a story to illustrate his point. While visiting a friend who had a child, he witnessed something puzzling. When it was time for any meal, the parents asked the child what *he* wanted for dinner, going as far as going to the supermarket at the last minute to fulfill their son's culinary whim. "I think it's really good for parents to be very encouraging and for children to have choices," he said. "But, I see more and more that people get carried away with this idea of choices. This abdication of responsibility was carried to the extreme when they asked their son, 'Do you want to go to school today or not?'" Predictably, Jerry explains that the boy has not done well. He called the shots growing up, but had a rude awakening out in the world. "In college, he was interested in the lectures but he definitely wasn't going to write papers. There's where freedom starts closing doors instead of opening them."

Troubling Situation #2: Leadership Without Acceptance

On the flip side is the parent who does see himself or herself as a leader, but has not embraced the all-important first step of acceptance, paying little attention to the individuality and needs of the family members. This type of parent, who is likely to demand unvarying adherence to rules, values, and morals, relies on control to get kids to behave. As we have seen, this breeds resentment and alienation and leads directly to the hamster wheel, where parents go round and round, addressing the same problems over again, never resolving the underlying issues. Sadly, children raised by this type of parent are likely to reject the values and morals that are forced on them.

Furthermore, with this type of parenting, there is little opportunity to guide kids to a positive expression of who they are. Jennifer Little, the parenting expert we met earlier in this book, spoke about reactionary "rules" or "consequences" to the child, and the almighty principle of "I'm the parent and I say so, so that's how it is." It is not constructive, she emphasized, especially when the CoreSelf is not addressed or accepted. Often, children of these parents don't feel like they're treated as separate human beings, with unique minds, personalities, and outlooks on the world.

I can personally relate to Jennifer's observation. I will be the first to admit that it is in my nature to speak up. I've always had strong ideas and the need to express them in words. In my family, I was seen as "bossy" and a "squeaky wheel," and I grew up ashamed of this part of who I am. Had the trait been accepted by my parents, instead of openly seen as something negative, hostile, and wrong, they might have shaped my behavior around it, rather than shaming me to "not be that way."

I wish that I had learned how to channel it more positively, and expressed it as *healthy*, constructive leadership. As it is, I have had a lifelong struggle balancing between flat-out telling people what to do versus having a healthy assertiveness. Perhaps there are aspects of your own personality that might have been channeled more productively.

Acceptance + Leadership Creates True Influence

By accepting who your child is, you create the strong, connected relationship that will empower you to concentrate your efforts on the thing you can change — your child's behavior. You will provide fertile ground for your positive influence. As we saw in Chapter 2, your child will care about what you think.

Your child will look to you for guidance. Your child will want your respect, and will want to please you. You can have a real, positive impact in your child's life. What better reward for all your commitment and dedication?

Contrast true influence with parental power, which comes from imposing your agenda on your child and finding a way to make him comply. This is the short-term solution that keeps parents on the hamster wheel. The experts agree. Dr. Michael Riera is an expert on understanding children and teenagers. His approach is based on the idea that, when children grow into adolescents, thinking in terms of influence is much more useful for parents than thinking in terms of control.[44] Alfie Kohn, author of *Unconditional Parenting*, echoes this, saying that when parents rely on power, they decrease their true influence.[45]

> Unlike the autocratic parent who insists on strict adherence to rules, the deeply bonded and connected parent is one the child will want to emulate.

Am I saying that if you lead with acceptance, your child will never misbehave? Of course not. Normal child development includes pulling away from parents, questioning values, and pushing limits. Sometimes, parents can't tell the difference between problematic behavior and healthy development. The CoreSelf model in leading with acceptance addresses it all, and gives parents the tools to help guide the behavior toward what is acceptable.

Remember the boy who didn't have to go to school from Jerry's example? He is certainly allowed to *try* to skip school.

But, there are lessons to be learned in being denied this request.

Your positive influence will extend far beyond shaping your child's behavior. When you strengthen the bond between you and your child through acceptance, you will be sharing your morals and values to a receptive audience. Unlike the autocratic parent who insists on strict adherence to rules, the deeply bonded and connected parent is one the child will want to emulate.

If You've Followed the Path to Acceptance, You're a Leader

As you worked through the steps in Part II, you drew on your leadership skills to understand and accept the Child You've Got. The steps required you to put the needs of your child before your own, become conscious, and take responsibility, all of which are characteristic of good leaders. Look particularly at being emotionally present. This commitment is not easy at times, and by providing this valuable direction, as you navigate everyday living and conflicts with your child, you are a leader. Enlistening also may require you to push yourself to do for your child what you might not do for yourself.

As I mentioned in the introduction, as Jordan's parents, Carl and I learned about the importance of leadership early on. Having made the commitment to accept Jordan's big, bold, bright, tenacious, relentless, strong CoreSelf, we found that "as Jordan goes, so goes the family." We realized that we needed to be strong leaders if we wanted to help Jordan develop into his best self.

When I was eight months pregnant with Ethan, my second child, Jordan was three years old. He was also, if you remember, tempestuous. One day little Jordan stood in front of me, put his arms around my legs and nestled his head into my huge, protruding belly.

My heart melted, because Jordan was not a touchy-feely, cuddly child. Yet, here he was, already embracing his little sibling! But, just as I began to relax into the lovely hug, Jordan did something shocking: he *bit* my belly!

Not a little nip; a real chomp. I recoiled in shock and pain. Beyond the physical hurt was the emotional "betrayal" I felt after relaxing into what I thought was a warm, sweet embrace. I shouted out and scolded him more angrily than I wished I had.

The bite surely got my attention, however. It was a cry for help, and I needed to get over my anger and step up as a leader by being emotionally present with the little boy who bit my belly. Unsure of what to do, I consulted with a child psychologist who had helped in the past with strategies to deal with my tenacious toddler. Kids are often terrified of what's in their mom's belly, she offered. No matter how much you try to prepare them, they can be very fearful. I left with a good idea of how I might help him through this scary and unsure time, at the same time teaching him not to hurt others.

During some connected one-on-one play after dinner, I said, "Hey, Jordan, I was wondering about something. You know how everyone keeps saying 'Aren't you excited? You're going to be a big brother!' Well, maybe you're not excited at all. I mean, maybe it's scary and you don't even know what it's going to be like, so maybe you're not excited. Maybe you're kind of worried."

I had his attention, and I continued. "I can understand it if you feel that way and it's perfectly okay. You don't have to be excited, or happy. You don't have to like the baby." His body visibly softened. "You feel however you feel! But you cannot hurt me, or anyone else. *Ever*. Do you understand?" He nodded and ran off.

A few weeks later, on the day we brought his baby brother home from the hospital, I noticed Jordan leaning over Ethan's cradle. I quietly walked up behind him to check out what he was doing. To my surprise — and joy! — he was gently patting the baby's back, softly cooing, "I'll always be here, baby."

And, he *was* always there for the baby. From day one, he was a wonderful older brother, something no one could have predicted based on his first three years. They remain best friends twenty-four years later. I am convinced that, by getting the help needed to understand Jordan's motivation, by allowing him to be terrified and anxious, and at the same time helping him manage these overwhelming feelings, we opened the door for him to access his loving, connected side. Without emotional presence, the harsh scolding would have been the thing he attached to his out-of-control feelings. Even if we had understood the underlying worry, what if our response had been, "There's no reason to worry. Everything will be fine. You're going to love your brother!"? By navigating that all-important middle ground between telling Jordan that he was wrong to feel such fear and completely ignoring his fear altogether, we were able to accept his intense feelings and teach him to *act* in a positive way. And that took leadership.

Influencing the Expression of CoreSelf Traits

"The traits of strong-willed children that drive many of us crazy can actually become strengths when we give our kids the understanding and guidance they need to head down the right path." — Robert J. MacKenzie, PhD

Teach your child to optimize who he or she is! That's really what you're doing when you accept their CoreSelf and guide them to become the best version of who they are. All children can be guided in this way, by teaching them to manage the challenges and maximize the opportunities inherent in each CoreSelf trait. Let's take a look back at the reframing we did in Chapter 6.

One aspect of a great leader is the ability to take a seemingly negative trait and spin it positively. For any parent-child relationship, this tactic can also teach the child how to view himself in this positive, confidence-building light, and this is what we are doing when we lead with acceptance.

For example:

- Your "stubborn" daughter refuses to get in the swimming pool for her swim lesson: "I like your strong determination. At the same time, however, you must pay attention to your swim teacher."

- Your "demanding" son wants you to buy him a toy and is throwing a fit at the store: "You know exactly what you want, don't you? I like that about you. At the same time, it is not okay for you to scream when you can't have what you want."

- Your "clingy" son does not want you to leave him with a babysitter: "I know you like to be with Mama all the time, and I love being with you, too. Sometimes though, I have to leave, so let's make sure one of your favorite sitters can stay with you."

- Your "wild" daughter is bothering other customers at a restaurant: "Your energy is great, but it's not appropriate to bother others by running around."

Cristina told me about her brother Danny. Although he's grown into a great young man, when he was growing up, he had what others called a "destructive personality." His strengths were his mechanical mind and his curiosity about how things worked. He would smash things to see what was inside, take apart his race cars, and grab at bees to see what they were. Once, the neighbor found him pouring sand into the pool — he just wanted to see what would happen.

One aspect of a great leader is the ability to take a seemingly negative trait and spin it positively.

Thankfully, Danny's parents found valuable, constructive ways to channel his energy and curious spirit, even though they admit it was a tiring, years-long process. They were leading with acceptance. Danny had high intensity, high activity level, low optimism, and high persistence. They recognized that, rather than making Danny wrong for being who he was, they needed to find appropriate outlets for his CoreSelf traits. For example, one way they fulfilled Danny's desire to see things taken apart and destroyed, while still setting limits on his destructive behavior, was to take him to environments where destruction was permitted: for example, monster truck rallies, recycling plants, and demolition of buildings. They shared these activities with him and let him know that they appreciated this part of him, but ultimately they taught him that, even though it might be fun to express feelings strongly, destroying property is wrong.

"Do not wish to be anything but what you are,
and try to be that perfectly." —St. Francis de Sales

Being a Leader — Even if You Think You're Not One

If you're not comfortable being a leader, this section is for you. All parents should do what they can to find it within themselves to develop the skills needed to be the head of their families. Learning to embrace your inner leader is doable — and crucial, especially if you have a strong-willed child. These children are sometimes difficult to understand and require the most guidance and leadership. Parents whose children control the family with their moods and desires are in for years of escalating helplessness if they don't step in and give these kids the guidance they need.

It's understandable that you might need some extra help in this department. After all, not everyone is a natural leader, much less comfortable with enforcing rules, establishing and following through with boundaries, or even adopting a stern tone to get a child to listen. Many people I've spoken to can't bear to appear even a little cross with their child. As one father put it, "A parent who is afraid of confrontation and will not step into that leadership role against a strong-willed child will have a problem starting to lead from somewhere healthy." Sometimes, circumstances beyond a parent's control create or inflate this fear of playing bad cop. For instance, a mom who has a hectic work schedule or travels frequently hardly wants those few precious moments she gets with her son to instead be full of reminders for him to do his homework, or fights over bedtime. This parent may fall into a pattern of avoiding confrontation with her child simply because she can't bear to be "negative" during the only time she spends with her child each day. In the short term, it's easier to push problems away than to assume that leadership role.

Parents whose children control the family with their moods and desires are in for years of escalating helplessness if they don't step in and give these kids the guidance they need.

Working with parents in workshops, I hear many questions like, "What's the difference between accepting my child and caving in?" or "What's being too harsh, and what's standing up for what you believe are good values?" Let me tell you — each circumstance has a different solution. It's a balancing act for many parents.

On the other hand, some parents may misinterpret their obligation to be a strong leader and tip the scales toward becoming bullies. It can be so easy — one minute you may think you're doing the right thing in urging your child out of his comfort zone, and, the next you find yourself ignoring who your child is and expecting them to be different. If this happens to you, you must find another way to lead that does not make your child feel ashamed or wrong for who he is. One particularly good book on the subject of being an authoritative parent rather than an authoritarian parent is *Raising an Emotionally Intelligent Child: The Heart of Parenting*, by John Gottman.[46]

Coaching can also be a big help to parents who need assistance in finding the right balance.

Helena, the mother of seventeen-year-old Aidan, whom we met earlier in this book, says that one of the most valuable ways she learned to be a parent who leads was realizing she was first a parent who *sacrifices*. Enforcing rules for Aidan, for instance, usually meant she was the one who had extra work.

"Sometimes, when you reprimand the kid or take stuff

away, you as the parent have to pay for it," she recalls, laughing. "If you take away a car, for instance, *you're* the one who has to end up driving him around. *You* have to suck it up and go, 'I'm back to driving him to school again…'"

Accepting that this is a fundamental element of being a parent who leads is one step in not only seeing yourself as a leader, but also in knowing what leadership looks like, day to day.

The next section offers specific ways you can couple leadership with acceptance in raising your child.

Leadership Toolbox for Parents

Here are six leadership tools to help you navigate the day-in and day-out reality of parenting. Go through the toolbox and reflect on what you are already incorporating and where you might step up your leadership. Remember, always start with acceptance: "I know how much you enjoy your computer. At the same time, you need to turn it off and get ready for bed."

1. Emphasize the family unit.

With acceptance as your starting point, your children will know that they are valued for being their unique selves. Now, make sure they also know that they are part of something bigger than themselves, an integral part of the family unit. Children, like adults, thrive when they feel they belong. A sense of belonging fosters cooperation, where everyone contributes to the common good.

Emphasize the community with family rules, guidelines, agreements, and mottos. Explore with your children the question of, "Who are we as a family?" Does your family have a family crest, for instance? Perhaps make it visible in the home, and teach the history and values behind it. Every time you share religious, cultural, and ethnic traditions in your family, it helps reinforce the interdependence of being part of a family.

One very effective way to promote the importance of the family is to make family dinners a priority. Given the weekday schedules of typical families, family dinner can be just 30 minutes together. Carve out the time and expect everyone to be there. ("On Mondays, Wednesdays, and Thursdays, we'll eat together between 6:30 and 7:00 p.m., and, on Sundays, we'll have family dinner with Grandma and Grandpa at 5:30. Please don't schedule anything that conflicts without talking to Dad or me first.")

Emphasizing the family teaches children that their actions affect others, and that they are accountable to the family for their actions. A child who dawdles and holds up the family every morning, for example, should be made aware of how her actions affect the rest of the family.

2. Set and communicate clear, consistent standards of behavior.

We're not talking about expectations of who your child should be; these are expectations of how your child should behave. Think about the work world. In order to do their job properly, employees need an informative job description, and it's up to the boss to provide it. Family leadership is no different. If you want your children to behave properly, let them know clearly what's expected of them. The more specific the better (as developmentally appropriate), so they can learn to make choices about their behavior. Starting with toddlers ("Hitting is not acceptable."), through the teen years ("We want you to text us your location."), make sure you clearly communicate how you expect your kids to behave. If your daughter's job is to clean the bathroom every week, make a checklist that she can refer to; include scrubbing the shower, sink, countertop and toilet, mopping the floor and whatever the other specific tasks are.

Consistency is a cornerstone of effective parental leadership. A child needs to know what is expected of him each and every day, so he can adapt his behavior accordingly. While some kids only have to be told once, it takes days, weeks, months, and sometimes years for others to learn how to channel their behavior constructively.

> ## Consistency is a cornerstone of effective parental leadership.

Jordan provides a good example of this. As a preschooler, he was obsessed with Ninja Turtle action figures, and, one day, we went to Target to let him pick out several with some birthday money he had received. After that day, he would want to buy toys every time we went to Target, and he would scream and cry when told no. His reaction was influenced by his low distractibility, high intensity, and high persistence, and it took several years of consistent limit setting for him to develop the self-control needed to not throw a tantrum when frustrated. By age six, when we were driving in the car, he would ask me to warn him if we were going to pass Target, so he could turn his head away. He found he could control himself better if he avoided seeing the sign!

3. Build in accountability.

Standards of behavior are essential, but ineffective unless coupled with accountability. Returning to the example of the working world, employees have tasks to complete, deadlines, and periodic performance reviews. If you're wondering why you have to nag your kids to do every chore, ask yourself whether you're holding them accountable. Set a specific deadline for completion, communicate it clearly, and check to make sure the job is done by the deadline. If you don't check to make sure your child has followed through, you may be encouraging noncompliance, because, if he knows you don't check, he has little incentive to do things he doesn't care to do.

If you have a rule that all toys in the family room must be put away before bed each night, but you end up doing it because you're too exhausted to battle the kids over this, there is no accountability. To be an effective leader, you must hold your kids accountable and not do the job yourself out of short-term expediency or an aversion to confrontation. Much to the chagrin of many parents I have spoken with, the commitment to holding kids accountable for following through can seem daunting. Yet it's crucial to be an effective leader and raise well-adjusted children.

A child who is taught at home to be kind to people might bully other kids at school. Why? Because he can. He gets away with it because his parents are not paying enough attention to hold him accountable for his behavior outside the home. This is where it might take some extra legwork to investigate what's going on. Remember "enlistening?" It is incumbent on parents to tune in to what is going on, by paying attention and responding to a teacher's or another parent's phone calls, or asking others for feedback.

4. Follow through with clearly communicated bottom-line consequences.

Employees are fired if they don't perform their job duties. When parents get fed up with having their requests ignored, they might wish they could fire their children! How many times have you seen parents warn their kids of some consequence if they don't behave and then not follow through? These parents are actually training their kids to ignore them, because, if there's no real bottom line, children will continue to do whatever they want to do, tuning out the constant nagging and threats. Set, communicate, and follow through with reasonable consequences for not completing a task. Children will learn about the consequences of their behavioral choices. ("It's noon, and the bathroom is not clean. Therefore, as we agreed, you will lose your TV time tonight. And tell your friend you can't come over until you finish your chores.")

If there's no real bottom line, children will continue to do whatever they want to do.

---

5. Use the language of leadership.

Words are profoundly powerful. In Chapter 6, we looked at how to reframe our perceptions of the Nine Traits of the CoreSelf by changing the descriptive words we used. Here, we are looking at the effectiveness of our messages about our children's behavior.

Leaders use "I" messages rather than "you" messages. "I" messages convey how you feel as a result of your child's behavior, rather than the spoken or unspoken blame that's inherent in "you" messages. The point of your communication is to influence your child's behavior, right? Which message is likely to get you the result you want?

- "Would you stop being so loud!" or
- "It frustrates me when I can't hear Grandma on the phone. Please go outside."

When you state the problem or issue without blame, you open the door for cooperation, and joint solutions. In the second example (the "I" message) your child might reply, "Can I stay here if I'm quiet?" *Win!* You've influenced your child's behavior in a positive direction. On the other hand, the "you" message—"Would you stop being so loud!"— is more accusatory and hostile, which invites defensiveness from your child.

If you need more motivation to shift into the "I" messages, imagine yourself at work. Your boss is unhappy with a report you've turned in. Which message would invite your cooperation to revise the report, and which would lead to negativity, feelings of inadequacy and hostility?

- "I need to see more backup support for your conclusion. Can you have it on my desk by Friday morning?" or
- "You messed up the report! Fix it by Friday morning."

My friend Jenny is a rock 'n roll queen who plays bass in a band and names the baked goods she sells after Led Zeppelin songs. Yet, as enthusiastic as she is playing and listening to music, she is too self-conscious to dance to it. Her reason surprised me: When she was seven years old, she told her mother (who was by all accounts a great mother), that she wanted to take ballet lessons.

"Oh, Jenny, you're about as graceful as an elephant!" her mom blurted out, and this comment was forever seared into

Jenny's consciousness. Perhaps Jenny's desire to dance triggered a painful psychological script for her mom, because she would never knowingly want to hurt her daughter. It had nothing to do with Jenny, but it wounded her deeply and has held her back from fully expressing herself, even as a grown, self-aware woman.

Jenny's story reminded me of my own mother's regrettable lapse. My given name is Nancy Jo. Frustrated with my temperament, she gave me the nicknames "Nasty Jo" and "Nancy No." How do you grow up feeling good about your assertiveness when it is framed in this way? You don't!

When you state the problem or issue without blame, you open the door for cooperation and joint solutions.

---

6. A leader must walk the walk, not just talk the talk.

Perhaps the most powerful tool of all in your leadership toolbox is your power to lead by example. One of the quickest ways to alienate an adolescent child is to be a hypocrite. This will absolutely grate on them and lead to contempt. Children will follow what you do, not what you say.

No matter what your rules or values are, you must be a pillar of support for your child. You must commit to nurturing him into the best person he can be.

Jacky Howell, the early childhood education expert we heard from earlier in this book, said that, when a child grows up in an environment where there are rules, regulations, and limitations, it is more constructive than a laissez-faire environment where children have little or no guidance.

"The idea that children do need someone who makes decisions — that something as simple as saying to a child, 'What would you like to wear today? Here are three outfits, pick *one*.' — is often forgotten by many new parents." She laughed, recalling many parents who almost bend over backwards out of love so a child can explore the outfits she wants to wear, or the foods she wants to eat, or the activities she wants to do for the day. However, this isn't fair to the parent — or the child. Teaching your child that *you* have a system of rules and a set schedule in order to keep your lives moving is invaluable. Jacky added, "I always say over and over again in my workshops, 'There is this word. It's *no*. Learn to say it.' You find more and more families are giving up the control, the decision-making, the leadership to children. As a result, that child will develop characteristics that can make things difficult for them later on in life. You need to make sure you have some safe and appropriate limits."

You need to step up to the helm and be a pillar of support for your child. Leading with acceptance means parenting with your child's CoreSelf in mind, helping him to recognize his own gifts and knowing the boundaries of challenging him.

*

As we've discussed throughout this book, acceptance is the starting point. Parents then use *their* wisdom and *their* values, not to tell the child who they must be, but to help the child become the best version of who they already are. Comfortable with who they are. Understanding who they are. Realistic about who they are. And a blessing in the world, which we'll look at in the final chapter.

Chapter 9: Leading with Acceptance Helps Everyone Thrive

"What's done to children, they will do to society."
— Karl Menninger

Throughout this book, you've heard from both children and adults whose lives are rich because of the acceptance their parents have shown them. The benefits of leading with acceptance start with the child, and then extend outward into the world, helping everyone thrive.

Giving Children License to Shine

As you learn to lead with acceptance, you give your children license to shine. Instead of growing up ashamed of their weaknesses, you help them become the best version of who they are. When children have been given the gifts of acceptance and guidance, they start life with a good, solid foundation to weather the storms of adolescence and growing up. If they've been accepted for who they are, they won't crave acceptance from others, always trying to fit in, so they'll be less susceptible to peer pressure. Because they're secure in their self-image, they're less likely to be the target of bullying. When their own unique preciousness is celebrated, they're in a good position to make wise choices when faced with typical teenage dangers. If they're supported at home by parents who lead, they will have resources to draw on within their family. A child who feels a deep connection with his parents will be less likely to smoke cigarettes or take drugs. A child who has a sanctuary at home will be less likely to be out on the streets getting into trouble. And when a child feels listened to by his parents, he's less likely to make impulsive decisions just to get out of the house, like getting married at eighteen just to escape from oppressive parents.

Parenting Peace of Mind

Leading with acceptance is not the easy way out. It means making your way through uncertainty and new challenges as you embrace this new way of parenting. You are the parents who will stand apart from the crowd when the crowd values things that will not help your children become their best selves. You are the parents who will have to find a way to stand strong when you realize that pressuring your child to be the Child You Want is the wrong path. You are the parents who will have pangs of insecurity when other parents make negative comments or when you see the résumés that other kids are racking up. But you will do what you need to do to lead with acceptance, because you understand that acceptance is a fundamental human need, and because you see the difference it's making in your child, in your family, and in you.

When you lead with acceptance, you reap a priceless benefit from your vision, commitment, and courage: parenting peace of mind. Your children respect and trust you and communicate with you. You avoid the hamster wheel that we've talked about many times in this book. The same hotspots are not flaring up repeatedly, because you make an ongoing effort to tune in to your child's CoreSelf and let your child be true to who he is. This is not to say that when parents lead with acceptance, all stress, sleepless nights, and angry confrontations will be eliminated. Of course, the normal ups and downs of child rearing will happen. But the endless battling that resulted from being disconnected and alienated from your children will be a thing of the past.

Rather than battling to control your child's every move, you can enjoy the influence that results from your strong connection. Your kids will come to you with their problems, and they will care about your opinion. When you and your child hit a rough patch, you'll have an underlying faith that you'll make it through, and an underlying belief that your child will tend to make good choices. Your children will be more likely to let you know in words when something is wrong, rather than by acting out, because they will have confidence that you want to know their feelings and you have the ability to handle their anxiety, anger, or insecurity.

When you lead with acceptance, you reap a priceless benefit from your vision, commitment, and courage: parenting peace of mind.

This gives a level of certainty to parenting that is welcome and refreshing. Your child knows that you have his back, are there for the long haul, and that you respect him enough to let him be who he is.

In return, your child cares about who you are and respects you for it. He sees you as human, as someone who, like himself, has a unique CoreSelf with challenges and opportunities associated with each trait. He understands the morals and values that you live by and want to pass along, and he's willing to consider your point of view, because you listen to his. Mutual respect is an essential component of your relationship.

You will gain peace of mind that, when your child is ready, she will leave the nest and find her way in the world. She won't be chasing after acceptance from the wrong crowd because she knows who she is, and she is realistic about her strengths and weaknesses. She knows that she has gifts to share with the world and she will find a way to do it.

Significantly, you will have peace of mind that, long after she is gone from the nest, you will continue to be important parts of each other's lives — by choice, not just because you're family.

Ending Toxic Legacies

As we have seen, everyone comes to the parenting table as the product of their own upbringing by their parents. Patterns of relating and psychological coping mechanisms are subconsciously passed down from generation to generation. What you received as a child, you give as a parent, and your children will, in turn, pass on if you don't break the legacy.

Toxic legacies can be broken.
Imagine putting an end to the pain that has
plagued generations of your family!

Now that you lead with acceptance, you have a technique for identifying the harmful beliefs that get in the way of accepting who your child is, and a framework for change as you travel the path to acceptance of your child. What you may not have been willing to do for yourself, you are willing to do for your child: to look inside yourself and face your pain and fears. Toxic legacies can be broken. Imagine putting an end to the pain that has plagued generations of your family! This shift can help you not only to change the future for your children, but also heal your own difficult relationships with your parents. With the openness and humility you gain from leading with acceptance, these seemingly insurmountable obstacles can be transformed.

Less Sibling Rivalry

One of the most common reasons brothers and sisters don't have good relationships is that they have to vie for their parents' attention, love, and acceptance. Under these conditions, why would they choose to be around each other if they don't have to?

When parents lead with acceptance, on the other hand, siblings are not in competition with each other, as each child's unique CoreSelf is understood and accepted. Does this make a difference in their long-term relationships? You bet!

Due to a lack of leadership from my parents, I was mocked mercilessly by one of my siblings — for stupid and quirky things, as is often the case: the way I held my pinky when I played the piano; my food preferences; the way my eyelids met when I slept. It should not have been tolerated in the first place, much less allowed to continue for years. So, I was sensitized early on to the importance of appreciating differences in siblings and not tolerating this type of teasing.

With my sons, when I would hear this type of seemingly minor put-down ("You're so weird! I can't believe you won't eat cream cheese!"), I would step in with, "We don't talk like that in this family. There are things about you that your brother might think are weird. We all are different and we all like different things." Again, these types of barbs might seem trivial on the surface, but they are not. They make a child feel that they are not as good as someone else, and that their differences are shameful. Importantly, they can lead to an escalating cycle of retaliation and put-downs. To avoid this, employ guidance that allows siblings to grow up appreciating and being respectful of each other's differences, which promotes closeness.

Growing Up and Giving Back

While interviewing people for this book, I noticed that so many of them have dedicated their lives to helping others. Upon talking with them, I found that they had indeed been raised with accepting parents who were respectful yet committed leaders.

Kevin Viner, the magician we met earlier in this book, acts as a mentor to a younger, aspiring magician. Unlike Kevin's parents, however, this young man's parents are not supportive of his love of magic and dream of becoming a professional entertainer. "His mom is extremely strict," Kevin explained. "She's saying, 'We don't want you doing magic; we want you to be a doctor.'" When he reached out to Kevin for advice, Kevin drew from his own experience to offer some perspective. "I said, 'At the end of the day, do what you really want to do. Parents are not always right. They try to look after our best interests, but they're not right one hundred percent of the time. You have to go after it because a) you wind up resentful, and b) you end up regretting it.'"

Kevin tries to open the young man's eyes to the value of a parent's wishes. Yet, he also knows the importance of following one's passion. The result: he's making a significant difference in this young man's life as he makes choices about his future.

Kate, a twenty-three-year-old behavioral therapist living in Southern California, is another example of someone who feels that her parents' acceptance and strong leadership helped her live her purpose and help others. She provides one-on-one behavior therapy to children with autism. "I grew up in a very supportive and understanding environment," Kate explained. "My parents always set ground rules, but were flexible in allowing me to follow the rules in my own way." She laughed, adding, "They still made me eat my veggies! They were keen on identifying my interests and assisted me in pursuing these interests. Likewise, they learned my weaknesses and took the time to help me overcome them."

One such challenge was her overly intense empathy, something that she has now moderated and turned into a strength, even though it was a difficult trait when she was young. "I felt the pain others felt. Instead of punishing me for being overly sensitive, they allowed me to explore my empathy and learn to control it in a way that would help me. They encouraged me to volunteer at a local animal shelter. The shelter was difficult for me because I didn't like seeing that the animals were cold and all by themselves in the kennels. But, other times, I learned that by simply being there and playing with them, I helped the animals be happy. I learned that, even though I can't change everything, I can help by being present in the moment and being positive. I believe my parents helped shape my empathy into something that is now a strength, and something I use every day working with special needs children."

Kate added, however, that she recognizes the challenges her parents must have confronted to ensure she had this transformative experience growing up. "Let me be clear," she began. "My mom is a lawyer, and my dad has his own business building elevators. My mom wanted me to go into business. When I told my parents I want to help people for a living, they said two things: First, helping others pays nothing. Second, they were proud of me, and, if this was what I wanted, they would help me in any way they could. This type of support from my parents has been a constant in my life and led to my career today."

The acceptance and willingness to guide that Kate's parents gave her mean that today she is helping many children. She says that, without her parents' guidance, she doubts she'd have the patience needed to truly make a difference in other children's lives. "Because of the services I provide, children who had no language skills are finally asking for the things they want. I am teaching children to brush their teeth, use the bathroom, and wash their hands. I am teaching children socially significant behavior that decreases their anxiety and increases their happiness. I believe I am doing what I was meant to do."

> One can't help but visualize the light building as more and more parents lead with acceptance and allow every child to shine. Just imagine the magnificence of this brilliant illumination.

Leading with acceptance reinforces the many blessings that come from feeling valued for who you are. Children grow up understanding that it just takes one person to make a huge difference in a person's life, and that they can be that person. They will find their natural place among others, confidently knowing what their strengths are. By accepting your child — as Kate's parents did — you are not only embracing your child's gifts, you are also granting others infinite access to your child's light.

How the World Benefits from Leading with Acceptance

Leading with acceptance helps one child at a time. It starts with giving one child license to shine by being who she is. No more hiding her light under a bushel. No need to play small. And, as that child moves out into the world, shining her own unique and precious light, it empowers others to do so as well. One can't help but visualize the light building as more and more parents lead with acceptance and allow every child to shine. Just imagine the magnificence of this brilliant illumination.

Leading with acceptance allows children's unique selves to blossom within the context of the world in which they live, as part of the greater whole. I can't think of a more wonderful vision for the future.

Payoffs for Families

It's no surprise that a happy child makes for a happy clan. Families who are led with acceptance enjoy spending time with each other. Children will hang out at home more. Home can be a peaceful place, with good, honest communication. All members of the family are more available to nurture relationships and support each other.

For Lauren, a mechanical engineer, her love for and her dedication to her family has always been her first priority.

She said, "For me, unconditional love and support does more than just help a child. It was through my parent's love for me that I learned how important it is to feel loved. I learned how much it mattered. And that, in turn, made me want to share that love with others, to go out and brighten others' days as best as I could."

Acceptance, however, is also a powerful attribute of families who are facing hardship.

Brian, now an aspiring stem cell medical researcher, had a difficult entrance into the world. His first memories are not of playing with peers on the playground — they are of recovering in hospitals.

"I was a baby born with severe tri-lateral cleft lip and palate, two inguinal hernias, dental and orthodontia issues, and bad eyes and ears. As I grew older, I had an inferiority complex due to the lack of acceptance from the majority of my young peers. I was awkward, and because of all of the surgeries and experiences, I had no connection with kids my age." Brian explained, however, that his strongest source of support was his grandmother. "In my life, I have not met anyone since who has so readily accepted strangers, put others before herself so selflessly, and cared so readily about her friends and loved ones, as demonstrated by the lengths she would go to take care of me, her family, and her friends."

Brian explained that his nana was his tether. She planned activities, introduced Brian to friends she knew would accept him, made lunch, and even overcame her fear of driving to take Brian to school as a child and ensure he was in good hands every single day. Brian attests that, because of the unconditional acceptance his nana demonstrated, he himself is an accepting, caring person who welcomes new friendships and experiences — even though he admits he could have easily become incredibly lonely, selfish, and bitter toward the world.

"Based on my previous experiences, one would think I have

little faith in the future of humanity, but because of the people I have met and the friendships I developed, I am more hopeful than ever of the kindness and love of people and still do all I can to help those in my life meet their goals and succeed in life."

It just takes one individual to question the status quo and rock the boat, in order to end the toxic legacy of lack of acceptance.

Brian's grandmother didn't simply tell him to accept others, she demonstrated its value each day. Acceptance not only of Brian's gifts and deficits but also his difficult situation made their relationship a huge source of love and support. Knowing that acceptance is a powerful tool is something that he brings with him to every single relationship and challenge.

How poetic that the very traits of my CoreSelf that triggered my mom (intense, big, bold, tenacious, questioning, and relentless) are the reasons I was able to make sense of what happened and find a way to stop it in its tracks. It just takes one individual to question the status quo and rock the boat, in order to end the toxic legacy of lack of acceptance.

I'm proud that I did that for my family. I've made mistakes along the way, and my sons have been the guinea pigs for their mother's need to make sense of it all.

One thing that's clear is that the acceptance that I write about is a journey, not a destination. With my sons, the journey gracefully unfolds and deepens, suddenly lurches forward, and then seems to stop in its tracks, like Mercury gone retrograde. They both know that I want to understand and accept who they are, and who they are becoming. I know that in their openness, they will express anger toward me, and it's not easy to hear. But it is as necessary as hearing their expressions of love and gratitude. And the pain surely keeps me from making too many grand proclamations about having all the answers.

All parents make mistakes. Although my mother's mistakes caused me great pain, what a blessing she has been in my life. When I was a new mother, she was able to foresee the troubles ahead if things didn't change, and she spoke up. "Nancy, he's just like you!" Without her, it might have taken years to understand, or I might not have ever understood the undesirable legacy that I might pass down to my beautiful baby.

Once I experienced my moment of grace and really understood what it must have felt like to her to raise me, she was willing to look at her role in our relationship, take responsibility for her actions that were hurtful and damaging, and shed painful tears of remorse. And with this humble openness came a side of her I hadn't known and might not have ever seen.

Our closeness has continued to grow, and she wholeheartedly supports me writing this book. As I travel along my healing, transformational path and share more openly with her, it has resulted in a sweet, trusting dialogue between us. When she revealed how lonely she gets at 9:00 p.m., I encouraged her to call me every night to connect, and that I would be available as much as possible. These nightly calls have continued for several years now, and, because we talk so frequently, the conversation has gotten deeper and more substantial, going beyond the obligatory catching up on the family and small talk. She realizes I am there to listen, that I have set aside the time, and I don't rush off the phone. I ask her questions about her life; she has started to relax and remember things she hasn't thought of in years. Forgotten pieces of her childhood have emerged, and she would explore her memories and her feelings with me.

She said she was shocked that I wanted to hear these things. I encouraged her by really listening, not judging, and showing genuine interest in what she had to say. She began to feel safe, revealing parts of herself that she had locked away for eight decades. Learning about her vulnerable, less than perfect qualities made her much more human and interesting to me. Our connection has grown and deepened. I feel blessed. Physical presence (our nightly phone call) and emotional presence (deep listening, not judging) have allowed me to see my mother in a way that I never did while I was growing up. I see her with fresh eyes. And through my eyes she is making peace with and accepting herself for who she is. And, guess what she now sees?

"You're just like me!"

When we began this nightly ritual, I worried that I was making myself vulnerable. Would I again feel like a burden? Would my old indignant rage be rekindled? Would she feed me her bullshit, like, "The sun came out when you were born," which was so incongruous with how she had "treated" me that it would set me off?

Yes, I was vulnerable, but when I opened up, it seemed to encourage her to share more of who she really was. And the more I accepted her for who she was, the more I noticed something shifting within me. I knew we had healed when she repeated, for the umpteenth time, "The sun came out when you were born," and, for the first time, *I believed her.*

And what of the feisty, bold boy of three who held me close and bit my belly containing his unborn baby brother? Jordan continues to inspire me as he navigates the world beyond our family. During a recent visit back home, while I was in the midst of writing this book, we reflected together about his childhood.

He realized that raising him couldn't have been easy. "You and Dad did a great job," he generously offered, and talked about his intensity, persistence, and outlook on life. "It couldn't have been easy," he said, and he thanked me. If I needed a reminder of the challenges and opportunities present in every child's CoreSelf, and the essential role of parental leadership, Jordan handed it to me at that moment. All children deserve the opportunity to become the best version of who they are. EVERYONE thrives when parents lead with acceptance.

Acknowledgments

When I began this book, I didn't realize it would be a love letter to my mother. Thank you, Mom, for having the courage and humility to look deep inside yourself, for helping me make sense of my life, and for ultimately accepting me for who I am. Our journey together has brought great meaning to my life.

I'm grateful to my amazing sons, Jordan and Ethan, for graciously allowing me to write about who they are in such a personal way. Writing about acceptance and living it are two different things, and both of you keep me honest in walking the walk.

My brothers and sisters, Mark, David, Ellen, and Jackie, have supported and trusted me as I set my version of our family life on paper. I appreciate the mutual respect, connection, love, and commitment we have to each other and to our family.

Without the incisive eye of Diane O'Connell, Editorial Director of *Write to Sell Your Book*, this book would not have come to fruition. Thank you, Diane, for helping me find my voice, develop my ideas, and expand my competence as a writer. Your superpower is working with first-time authors and it is my super good fortune to have worked with you!

Executive Editor Cristina Schreil, also at *Write to Sell Your Book*, provided essential research and writing assistance. Cristina, thank you for helping me flesh out my ideas and for your saint-like patience with my slow learning curve on Microsoft Word. You were there when I needed help, and this book is so much better because of your contributions.

Two writers welcomed me into their world with a sweet generosity of spirit, and I want to make sure they know how much it meant to me. Gary Silva, a former Poet Laureate of Napa Valley and Professor at Napa Valley College, offered to help in any way I needed, saying, "We writers need to support each other." Hearing him call me a writer sent chills up my spine! Paul Chutkow, an accomplished author, journalist, and publisher, has supported and encouraged my work from the moment I first drew him a diagram outlining how to give children license to shine.

Dorothy Carico Smith walked into my life through Paul, and elevated my work to another level with her brilliant cover design and collaboration. You can now find her influence everywhere in my work, as she has become an essential member of my team.

I consider myself a speaker first, and Betsy Strauss and Vince Nash are two friends who convinced me to write a book. Thank you both for your confidence that I could do it and for your wisdom about reaching out to a wider audience to spread the message of acceptance.

Gail Larsen of Transformational Speaking, insisted that I show more of myself in my speaking, which helped me show more of myself in my writing as well. "Bigger, Nancy, *bigger!*" she pushed.

Beth Dana intuitively knew I was a healer since the day we

synchronistically met, long before I had an inkling. She has had a great influence on my professional direction.

Ruth King's work on the disguises of rage is both brilliant and practical, and working with her was transformational. I hope that this book helps people in the way that Ruth's book, *Healing Rage*, helped me. To the "raging beauties," (you know who you are) we will always be connected by our journey together.

Nancy Kaplan, Jeanette Valassopoulos, Purvi Parakh, and Terri Leasor have been my cheerleaders throughout every step of the writing process, and Za Fetterly gave me valuable early help in shaping my message.

Thank you, Janice Tres and Sabine Hirsohn from Sunrise Montessori of Napa Valley, for giving me an early platform to share the ideas in this book. Kristina Seher of the Principled Academy, also an early supporter, asked me to adapt leading with acceptance for classroom teachers, and her confidence and guidance have been a blessing.

My brother David has connected me with so many like-minded people that I call him my "bragent." Thank you, David.

To every client and friend who trusted me to coach them through their parenting issues, I appreciate your confidence in my work. This book would not have been possible without your contributions.

I spent two and a half years writing, and I could not have managed this without the strategic advice provided by Scott Schwartz, my financial planner and trusted advisor.

Heartfelt hugs go out to all of my precious friends for the love and connection we share, and to the many healers who have shared their gifts and helped me on my path.

Finally, an enormous thank you to all the people who shared their stories in this book. Your truth will set many children free.

APPENDIX

Exercise: Who Do You See
When You Look at Your Child?

By Tamsen Firestone, Founder of PsychAlive.org
Adapted from http://www.psychalive.org/2011/08/who-do-you-see-when-you-look-at-your-child/

How well do I really know my child? What are the specific interests, passions, qualities, quirks, idiosyncrasies, and flaws that make up this particular person? The following questionnaire is designed to help you answer these questions.

Instructions: Think about your child and answer the following questions. Do not discuss the questions with your child or ask him/her for the answers. The answers must come from your observations of the child. If you don't have an answer, then observe him/her more carefully.

Think about these questions before answering them. Don't give an automatic answer (like: She's so defiant! He's unappreciative!). Don't just answer from your experience with him or her. Don't answer from the experience of your own childhood. Try to imagine how he or she is experiencing life; what it must be like being him or her. Don't rush through the list of question; take time to ponder whatever thoughts are stimulated by them. Allow yourself to wonder about why your child feels a certain way. Allow yourself to feel for your child in his or her life.

A Baby, Toddler or Pre-schooler:

Child: Name, Age, Sex _____

_____

What are your child's favorite activities? _____

_____

What makes him/her laugh? _____

_____

What is his/her favorite book? _____

_____

What is his/her favorite song? _____

_____

What is his/her favorite movie? _____

_____

What is his/her favorite toy? _____

_____

What is his/her favorite game? _____

_____

How does your child feel with the members of your family?

_____

_____

Who does he/she like? _____

_____

Who does he/she go to easily? _____

_____

Who does he/she shy away from? _____

_____

Who is he/she jealous of? _____

_____

How does he/she feel with your partner? _____

_____

How does he/she feel with you?_____

_____

Does he/she prefer one of you over the other? _____

_____

How does your child feel about him/herself? _____

_____

Is he/she critical of him/herself in anyway?_____

_____

Does he/she feel self-conscious in any situation? _____

_____

Does he/she ever feel shy? _____

_____

Does he/she ever feel afraid? _____

_____

When he/she has nightmares, what are they about? _____

_____

What are his/her thoughts about death? _____

_____

Write a description of your child.
When describing this young child, think about the traits
that you are enjoying seeing emerge in his/her personality.
To maintain objectivity, don't refer to him/her as your son/
daughter or child. When you are writing this, just refer to
him/her by his/her name.

_____

_____

_____

_____

_____

_____

_____

A School-age Child:

Child: Name, Age, Sex _____

_____

What are your child's interests? _____

_____

Which interests are the same as yours? _____

_____

Which are different; interests that you couldn't dream of sharing in a million years? _____

_____

Which are the same as your partner's interests? _____

_____

Which are different from both yours and your partner's; unlike anyone else's in the family? _____

_____

Which interests do you feel good about?_____

_____

Which do you feel uncomfortable with or disapprove of? ___

_____

Do you consider any to be a waste of your child's time? If so,
why?_____

_____

How does your child feel in the family? _____

_____

At what times in his/her childhood has he/she been happy?

_____

_____

What were the circumstances that made him/her happy?

_____

_____

At what times has he/she been sad, withdrawn, depressed?

_____

_____

What were the circumstances that made him/her unhappy?

_____

_____

How does he/she seem to feel now?_____

_____

What are the circumstances that are causing this today?

_____

_____

How does your child feel with the members of your family?

_____

_____

Who does he/she like to hang out with? _____

_____

Who does he/she joke around with? _____

_____

Who does he/she confide in and talk personally to? _____

_____

Who does he/she get into fights with?_____

_____

Who is he/she jealous of? _____

_____

Who does he/she feel uncomfortable with?_____

_____

Who does he/she avoid? _____

_____

How does he/she feel about your partner? _____

_____

How does he/she feel about you? _____

_____

How does he/she feel about your and your partner's relationship with each other?_____

_____

How does your child feel outside of the family? _____

_____

Does he/she have friends? Are they nice to each other?_____

_____

Does he/she like school? _____

_____

Does he/she feel comfortable with his/her peers? _____

_____

Does he/she feel self-conscious at school?_____

_____

How is he/she doing academically? _____

_____

What subjects does he/she have trouble with? _____

_____

What subjects does he/she like?_____

_____

Are there any subjects that he/she has a special enthusiasm for? _____

_____

Are there any situations at school that are bothering him/her?

_____

_____

If this applies: How does your child feel with girls/boys? ____

_____

Is he/she dating? _____

_____

Does he/she feel comfortable with girls/boys?_____

_____

Does he/she feel self-conscious and ill-at-ease with boys/girls?

_____

_____

Is he/she in a sexual relationship? _____

_____

How does he/she feel about him/herself sexually? _____

_____

How does your child feel about him/herself? _____

_____

Does he/she feel insecure in any way? _____

_____

Is he/she critical about anything about him/herself?_____

_____

What are his/her self-attacks? _____

_____

What are the personal limitations that he/she struggles with?

_____

_____

What are his/her thoughts about death? _____

_____

Write a description of your child.

Try to write it as an objective, compassionate observer. Don't
refer to him/her as your son/daughter or child. When you are
writing this, just refer to him/her by his/her name.

_____

_____

_____

_____

_____

Endnotes

1 Note that Maslow did not actually design this as a pyramid; this design came later when it was adapted by others. Maslow's version had the needs stacked on top of each other in a pillar.

2 Kim John Payne and Lisa M. Ross. *Simplicity Parenting: Using the Extraordinary Power of Less to Raise Calmer, Happier, and More Secure Kids* (New York: Ballantine, 2010).

3 Alexandra Robbins. *The Overachievers: The Secret Lives of Driven Kids* (New York: Hyperion, 2007), 113.

4 Madeline Levine. *Teach Your Children Well: Parenting for Authentic Success* (New York: Harper, 2012), 297.

5 Robert Frick. "Accepting Children (and Yourself and Everyone Else)," *Accepting and Appreciating Idiosyncracies,* [sic]. <http://www.rfrick.info/accept.htm>.

6 Haim G. Ginott, Alice Ginott, and H. Wallace Goddard. *Between Parent and Child* (New York: Random House, 2004), 8.

7 A review of Literature Supporting the Parenting by Connection Approach: At-a-Glance Summary, Rebecca Aced-Molina, M.A., <http://www.handinhandparenting.org/uploads/LitReviewOverview.pdf>.

8 CASAColumbia. *The Importance of Family Dinners VIII*, (New York: The National Center on Addiction and Substance Abuse at Columbia University, 2012).

9 Thomas Gordon. *Teaching Children Self-Discipline at Home and at School* (New York: Crown Publishing, 1989), 74.

10 Marianne Williamson. *A Return to Love: Reflections on the Principles of "A Course in Miracles"* (New York: Harper, 1996).

11 Joseph Campbell, Bill D. Moyers, and Betty S. Flowers. *The Power of Myth* (New York: Anchor, 1991).

12 Herman Hesse. *Siddhartha: An Indian Poem* (New York: Random House, 2006), 58.

13 Robert Holden. *Happiness Now!: Timeless Wisdom for Feeling Good Fast* (Carlsbad, CA: Hay House, 2007).

14 Alice Miller. *The Drama of the Gifted Child: The Search for the True Self* (New York: Basic Books, 30 Anv. Rev.Edition, 2008), 30.

15 Richard Weissbourd. *The Parents We Mean To Be: How Well-Intentioned Adults Undermine Children's Moral and Emotional Development* (New York: Houghton Mifflin Harcourt, 2009).

16 Wendy Mogel. *The Blessing of a Skinned Knee: Using Jewish Teachings to Raise Self-Reliant Children* (New York: Penguin Putnam, 2001), 43.

17 Wendy Mogel. *The Blessing of a B Minus: Using Jewish Teachings to Raise Resilient Teenagers* (New York: Scribner, 2010), 18.

18 Pema Chodron. *The Wisdom of No Escape and the Path of Loving Kindness* (Boston: Shambhala Publications, 2001).

19 Tamsen Firestone. "Who Do You See When You Look at Your Child?" *PsychAlive*. <http://www.psychalive.org/2011/08/who-do-you-see-when-you-look-at-your-child/>

20 Shunryu Suzuki. *Zen Mind, Beginner's Mind* (Boston: Shambhala, 2010), 1.

21 Rachel Simmons. *The Curse of the Good Girl: Raising Authentic Girls with Courage and Confidence* (New York: Penguin, 2009).

22 Mark Goulston. "What Your Teenager Wants You to Know But Won't Tell You." Weblog post. *Road Back From Hell Blog*. MarkGoulston.com, 17 Feb. 2011. <http://www.markgoulston.com/road-back-from-hell-what-your-teenager-wants-you-to-know-but-wont-tell-you/>.

23 Julianne Idleman. "Parent-Child Connectedness Takes Us Beyond Emotional Intelligence." Weblog post, 30 Nov. 2011, <http://www.handinhandparenting.org/2011/11/30/parent-child-connectedness-takes-us-beyond-emotional-intelligence/>.

24 ETR literature review of over 600 studies. Nicole Lezin, MPPM, Lori A. Rolleri, MSW, MPH, Steve Bean, MAT, Julie Taylor, BA. Parent-Child Connectedness: Implications for Research, Interventions, and Positive Impacts on Adolescent Health, ETR Associates, 2004.

25 Maggie Day Conran. "Loud and Clear." Weblog post. *Just Say No to Mommy Brain*. Blogspot, 17 Jan. 2012. <http://nomommybrain. blogspot.com/2012/01/loud-and-clear.html>.

26 Alexander Thomas; Stella Chess; Richard Lerner; Jacqueline Lerner, 1998, "New York Longitudinal Study, 1956-1988", <http://hdl.handle.net/1902.1/01126 Murray Research Archive [Distributor] V2 [Version]>.

27 Since the level of any trait, in and of itself, is neither good nor bad, I have renamed some of the traits to avoid judgment. Then show the table.

CORESELF TRAIT	THOMAS AND CHESS TRAIT
Activity	Activity
Adaptability	Adaptability
Distractibility	Distractibility
Intensity	Intensity
Ease with the Unfamiliar	Approach/Withdrawal
Optimism	Mood
Persistence	Persistence
Regularity	Rhythmicity
Sensory Reactivity	Sensitivity

28 The Myers-Briggs Temperament Indicator can be very helpful for parents. I prefer to use the Nine Traits model because 1) it assesses the level of trait on a spectrum, unlike Myers-Briggs, and 2) the nine traits are identifiable by two to three months of age, whereas Myers-Briggs is not effective until a child is about six years old, at the earliest.

29 Michael Gurian. *Nurture the Nature: Understanding and Supporting Your Child's Unique Core Personality* (New York: Jossey-Bass, 2007)

30 These are not the *only* inborn traits. The CoreSelf looks at *temperment* traits only.

31 Kim John Payne and Lisa M Ross. *Simplicity Parenting.*

32 Thomas and Chess use the concept of "goodness of fit" to describe how the traits of parent and child align with each other. Goodness of fit occurs when there is congruence between the parents' expectations and temperament and the child's temperament, interests, and abilities.

33 Robert Brooks, PhD. "Differences from Birth — Part I." Weblog post. *Dr.RobertBrooks.com*. Feb. 2000, <http://www.drrobertbrooks.com/monthly_articles/0002>.

34 Susan Cain. *Quiet: The Power of Introverts in a World That Can't Stop Talking* (New York: Crown, 2012).

35 Madeline Levine. "Amy Chua's 'Tiger Mother' Style Has Flaws." *SFGate*. 24 Jan. 2011. <http://www.sfgate.com/opinion/openforum/article/Amy-Chua-s-Tiger-Mother-style-has-flaws-2477937.php#photo-2040181>.

36 ibid.

37 <http://www.challengesuccess.org>.

38 Carl Pickhardt. "Surviving (Your Child's) Adolescence." *Psychology Today*. 21 Feb. 2011. <http://www.psychologytoday.com/blog/surviving-your-childs-adolescence/201102/vanity-parenting-and-adolescent-performance>.

39 <http://www.greatday.com/motivate/020716.html>. Copyright Ralph Marston 2002

40 Brené Brown. *Daring Greatly: How the Courage to Be Vulnerable Transforms the Way We Live, Love, Parent, and Lead* (New York: Gotham, 2012).

41 Gabrielle Roth developed the 5Rhythms (flowing, staccato, chaos, lyrical and still) in the 1970's. For more information, visit <http://www.5rhythms.com/>.

42 Wendy Mogel. *The Blessing of a Skinned Knee*, 49.

43 Naomi Aldort. *Raising Our Children, Raising Ourselves*. (Bothell,WA: Book Publishers Network, 2005), 79–80.

44 Michael Riera. *Uncommon Sense for Parents with Teenagers* (New York: Crown, 1995), 21.

45 Alfie Kohn. *Unconditional Parenting: Moving from Rewards and Punishments to Love and Reason* (New York: Atria Books 2006), 68.

46 John Gottman. *Raising an Emotionally Intelligent Child: The Heart of Parenting* (New York: Simon & Schuster 1997).

47 My mother cries at the thought of how hurtful her words were. She is a remarkable woman, and I am blessed to have had the opportunity to heal with her.

Index

A Note from the Author

Dear Reader,

Thank you for reading *Raise the Child You've Got— Not the One You Want*.

I invite you to share your feedback. Here are some suggestions:

- Post a review at amazon.com, barnesandnoble.com, and/ or goodreads.com.
- Comment on my blog at www.nancyjrose.com/blog.
- Let your favorite parenting bloggers know about the book.

I appreciate every small step you take to help spread the word about leading with acceptance.

In gratitude,

Nancy Rose

Made in the USA
San Bernardino, CA
30 July 2014